Mastering the Lap Steel Guitar

by Rob Haines

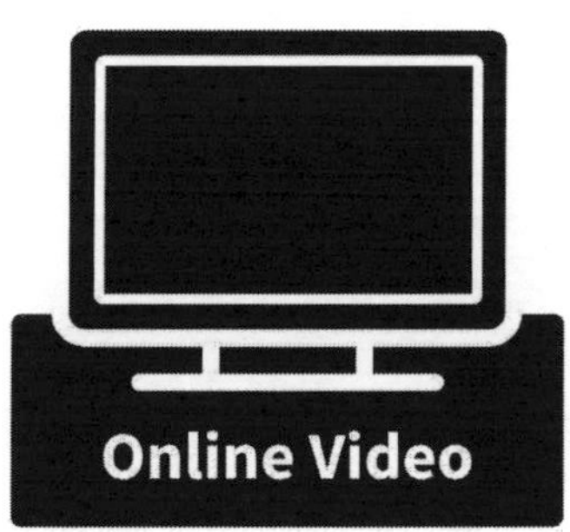

YouTube
www.melbay.com/30524V

Video
dv.melbay.com/30524

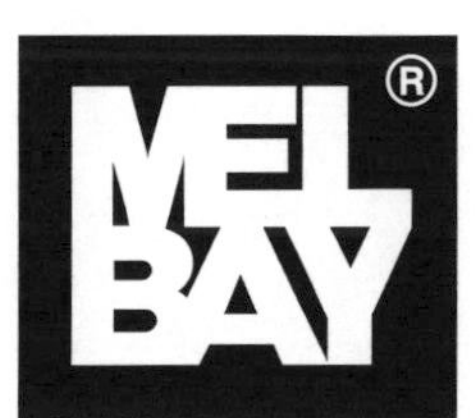

Visit us on the Web at www.melbay.com — E-mail us at email@melbay.com

Contents

Introduction

The lap steel guitar was invented in 1885. A seven-year old boy was walking along a railroad track and picked up a metal bolt; he slid the metal along the strings of his guitar and was intrigued by the sound. He taught himself to play in this style using the back of a knife blade as a steel. The instrument became popular in the United States during the 1920s and 1930s and was especially popular in Hawaii.

The lap steel guitar was electrified in the early 1930s, and in 1932 the first production electric model was introduced, the aluminum Rickenbacker A22 "Frying Pan" lap steel.

The lap steel guitar is also called a **non-pedal steel guitar**. A non-pedal steel guitar with legs is known as a **console steel guitar**. These are all basically the same instrument, with differing numbers of strings and necks. This book and video teaches the C6 tuning which is the most common tuning for an eight-string instrument. You can use a six string steel guitar; you just won't have the bottom two strings, the low A and F. It is the same tuning used on most C6 pedal steel guitars just without the pedals. Usually a C6 pedal steel guitar has ten strings, and there are some lap steels that have ten strings as well.

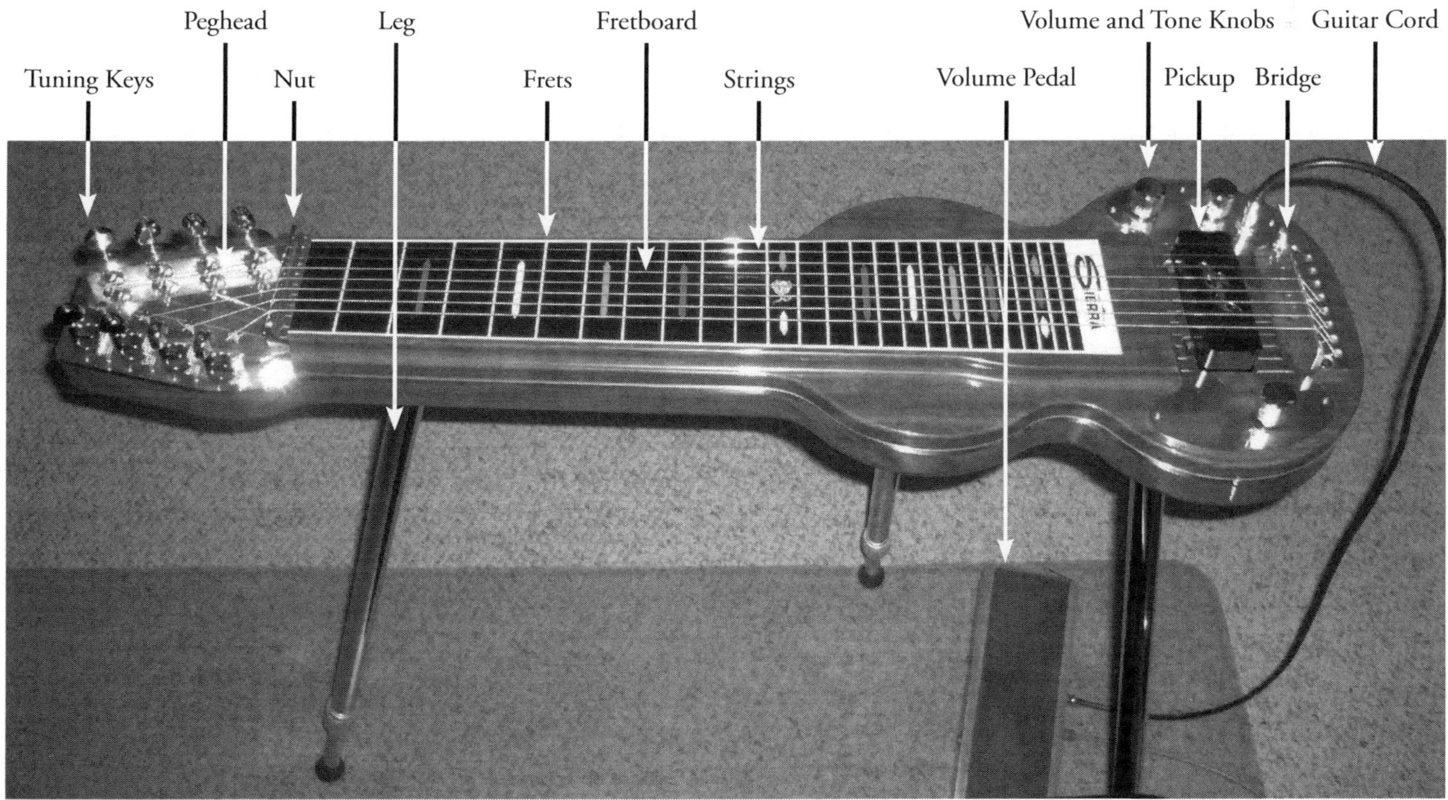

Please note that some parts have multiple names. For instance the peghead is also called the **headstock**. The tuning keys are also called **tuners**. In addition, the frets are not traditional frets like a guitar or mandolin has; they are painted on or simply flat graphics, but they are still called "frets." Some lap steels have multiple volume and/or tone knobs; some do not have any. It depends on the manufacturer.

Volume Pedal

Any volume pedal will do to get started, but at some point you will need a volume pedal that is designed to be used with a steel guitar. Manufacturers such as Goodrich, Hilton and Sho-Bud all make quality lap steel volume pedals. Avoid those that guitar players use, such as Ernie Ball, Dunlop and Morley.

Strings

Most lap steel players use a C6 set meant for a pedal steel guitar and simply discard the unneeded low strings. This is fine until you want to use a technique called **string pulling**. The gauges can be hard to pull. Here are the gauges that I use:

From top (highest pitch) to bottom (lowest pitch) –

1st	G .012
2nd	E .012
3rd	C .017
4th	A .020 plain
5th	G .024 wound
6th	E .030
7th	C .036
8th	A .042

Note that the 4th string A is plain. On some pedal steel sets it is wound. To do string pulls you will need this string to be plain. You might need to tweak the gauges according to the scale of your guitar.

Tuning 

Use an electronic tuner to get started in tuning your lap steel. Any kind of tuner will do. There are free smart phone apps to tune with as well. On my phone, I use the Pano Tuner.

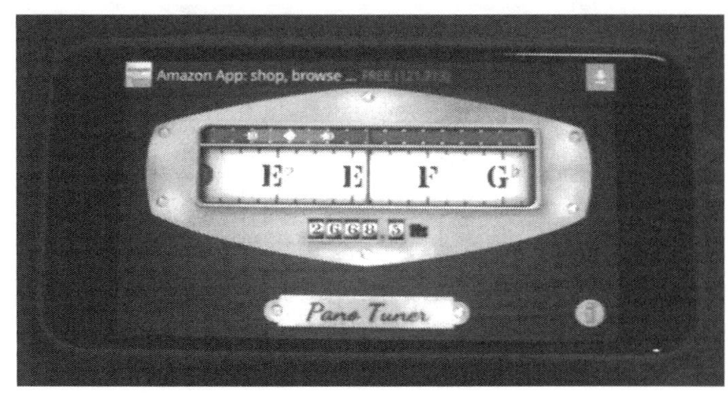

Using an electric tuner, tune the strings up to pitch EXCEPT for the E strings. They need to be tuned flat or below pitch. Hit the C and the E together and tune the E until the "beating" stops. This aspect of tuning is covered in more detail in the video where I will also show you how to tune using harmonics and other advanced tuning techniques.

The Bar 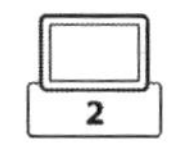

There are lots of different bars with varying diameters, lengths and weights. The most common bar I see is 7/8 inch in diameter and 3 and 3/8 inches in length (on the right in photo). I use this steel on pedal steel and it should work for you as well. But to help with bar slants, I use a larger bar on lap steel, 1 inch in diameter and 3 and ½ inches long (on the left). Stainless steel is the material of choice. The Stevens bar that Dobro® players use won't work in this situation.

Picks

Use a plastic thumb pick and metal fingerpicks. Picks need to fit snugly so they don't slide around and fall off. They will seem uncomfortable at first, but you will get used to it. I like the tip of the thumb pick to be thick. A small or pointed thumb pick will give you a thin sound.

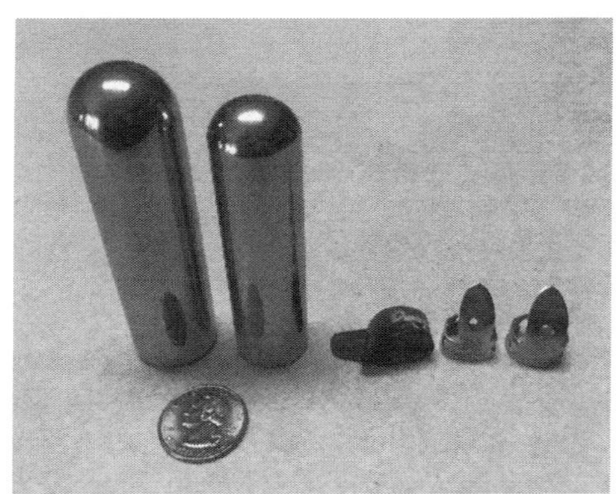

Standard Notation, reading music

A lot of steel guitar players don't read music, and use tablature instead. This book contains both standard notation and tab. Just study both as you work through this lesson, and the standard notation will eventually make sense. Here's a list of note and rest values to get started.

Table of Notes and Rests

Whole Note	𝅝	Whole Rest	𝄻
Half Note	𝅗𝅥	Half Rest	𝄼
Quarter Note	♩	Quarter Rest	𝄽
Eighth Note	♪	Eighth Rest	𝄾
Sixteenth Note	𝅘𝅥𝅯	Sixteenth Rest	𝄿

Time Signatures

The number on top indicates the number of beats in a measure. The number on the bottom represents the type of note that gets one beat.

4/4	The measure has 4 beats; a quarter note gets one beat.	2/4	
C	Common time, another way of writing 4/4	2/2 ¢	Cut time
3/4	Waltz time	6/8	

A **key signature** is a group of sharps or flats placed at the beginning of the staff. It shows the player which notes are to be played as sharps or flats throughout the piece. Don't get hung up with the rarely used key signatures, those with a lot of sharps or flats. The most common key signatures are fairly easy.

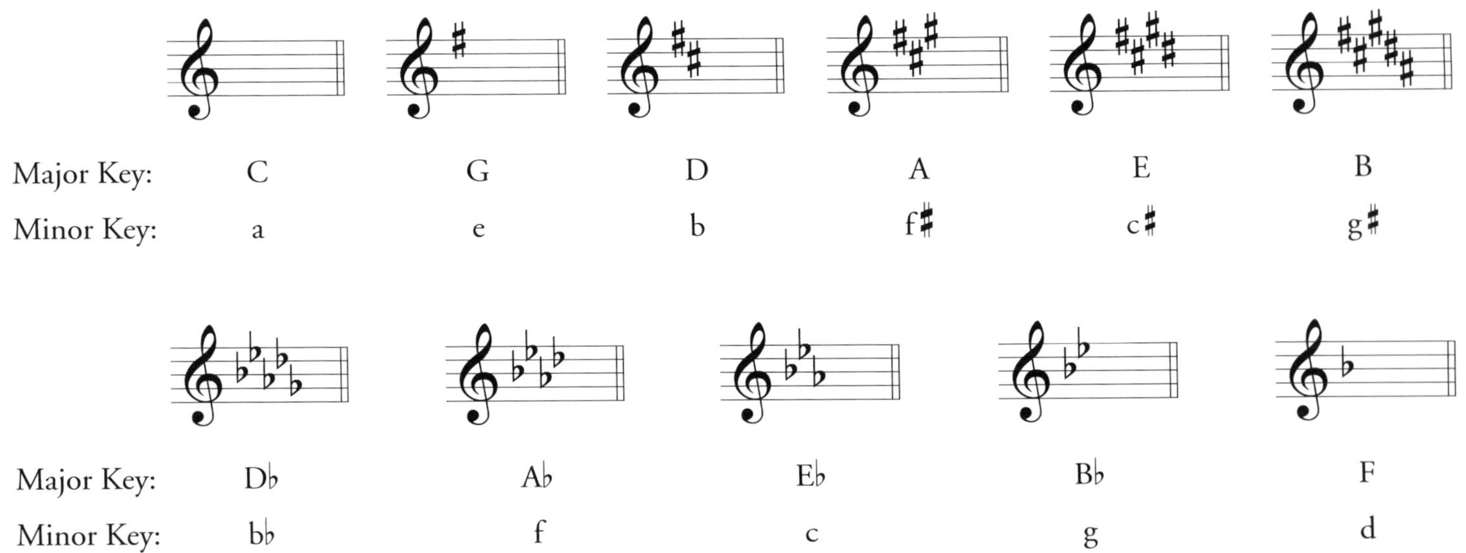

Right-hand blocking or **muting** is a way of making sure that the notes that you are playing don't just ring out. There are a couple of ways of doing this. Palm blocking involves bouncing your palm and damping the notes. "Pick blocking" means that as soon as you hit a note or shortly after hitting the note, the finger that played the note falls back down on the string to block or damp it. These techniques along with **left-hand technique** are covered in the video.

Vibrato is an effect consisting of a regular, pulsating change of pitch. It is used to add expression. This technique is covered in the video as well.

Lap steel guitars were manufactured by Epiphone, Gibson and National in the 1930s to cash in on the craze for Hawaiian music. Fender and Gretsch also produced lap steel guitars, but not until the 1940s. Because so many were made, it's easy to find these vintage instruments at a reasonable price.

National lap steels were made from 1935 until 1968, when the company went bankrupt. This model is called the New Yorker. The body has a "skyscraper" look.

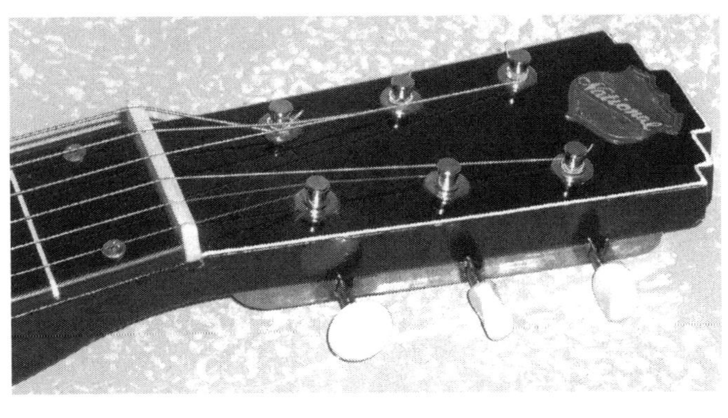

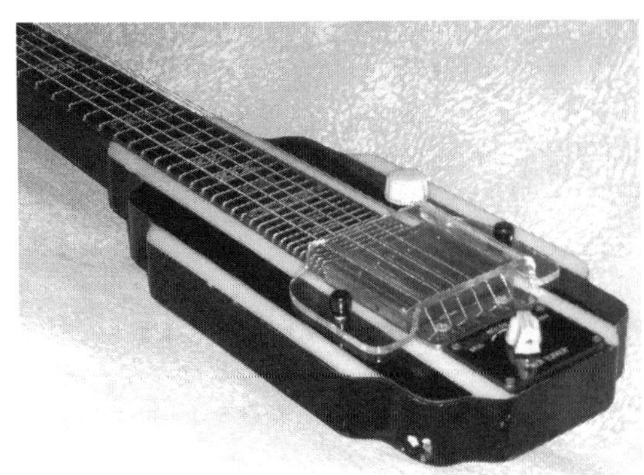

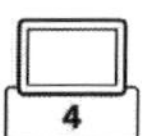

The C Major Scale Using Open Strings in the First Position

Note that the key signature for C major has no sharps or flats. Think of a piano keyboard; the C major scale uses all white keys, from C to C, with the natural half tone E-F and B-C. Notice the note names in the scale listed above the staff and their number in the scale. It is the location of the half tones between the 3rd and 4th and 7th and 8th scale degrees that gives the C scale its "major" quality.

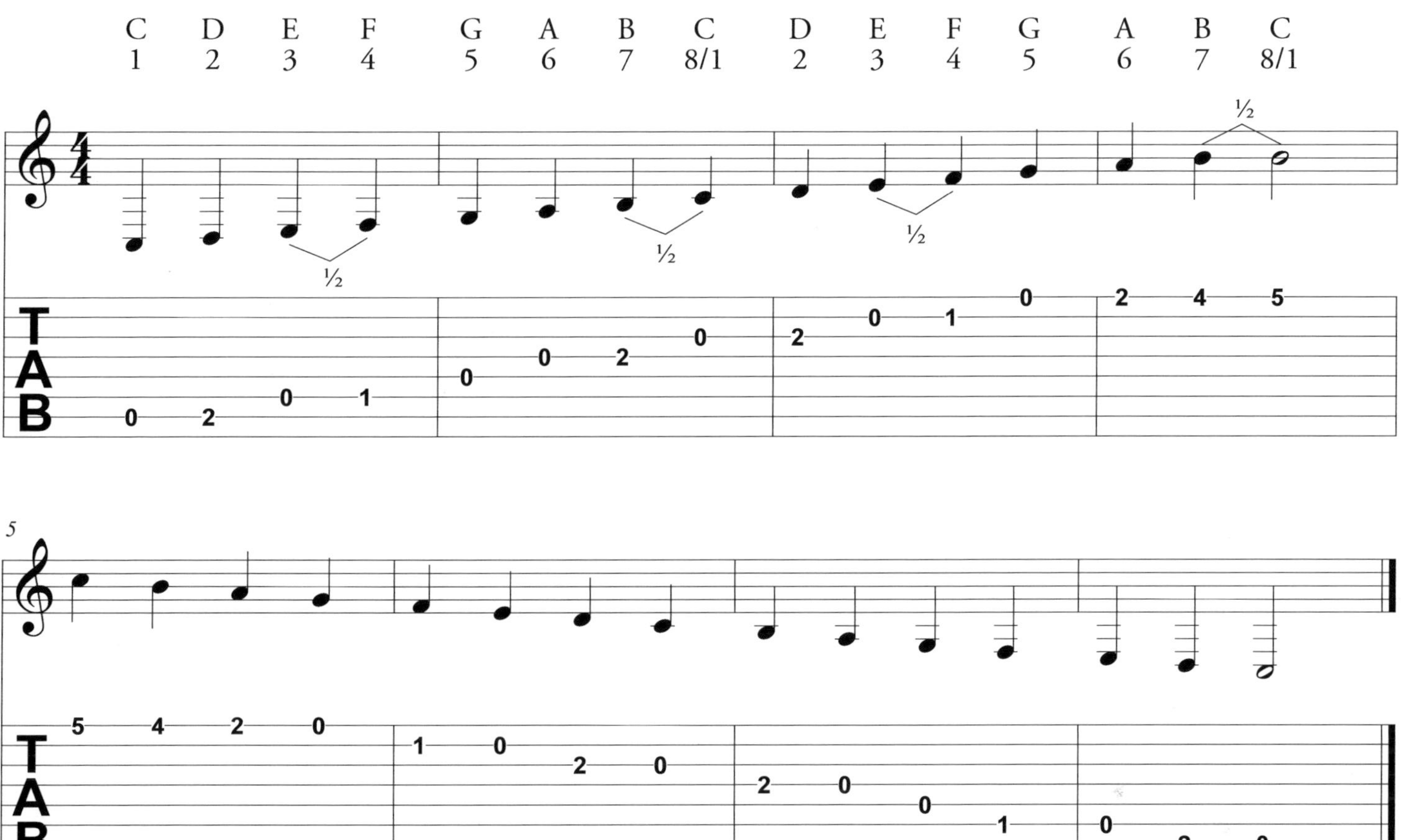

Here's an exercise where you play the notes of the open C^6 chord while sliding up on the adjacent lower string to play in unison. Work on playing in time, sliding smoothly and ending up in tune.

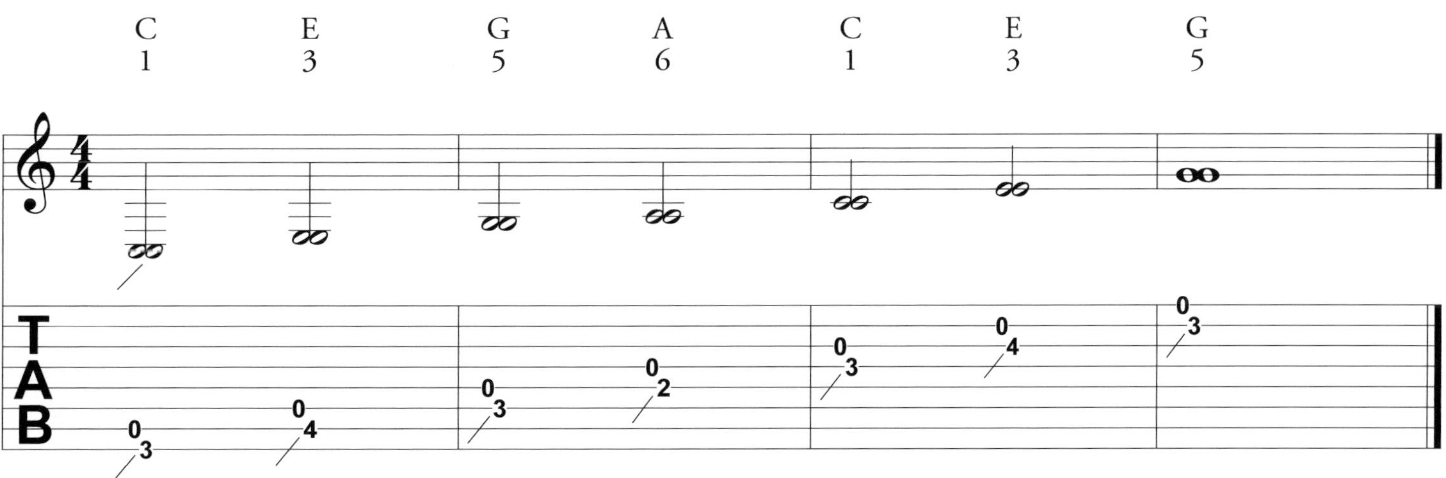

From the previous exercise, you can see that a major chord consists of the 1st, 3rd and 5th notes of the major scale. Hence, a C major chord is formed by the notes C, E and G. Add the 6th note, A, and you have the C^6 chord.

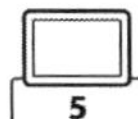

The G Major Scale

Note the key signature in the key of G major, one sharp. All of the F notes are sharp, placing the half tones appropriately.

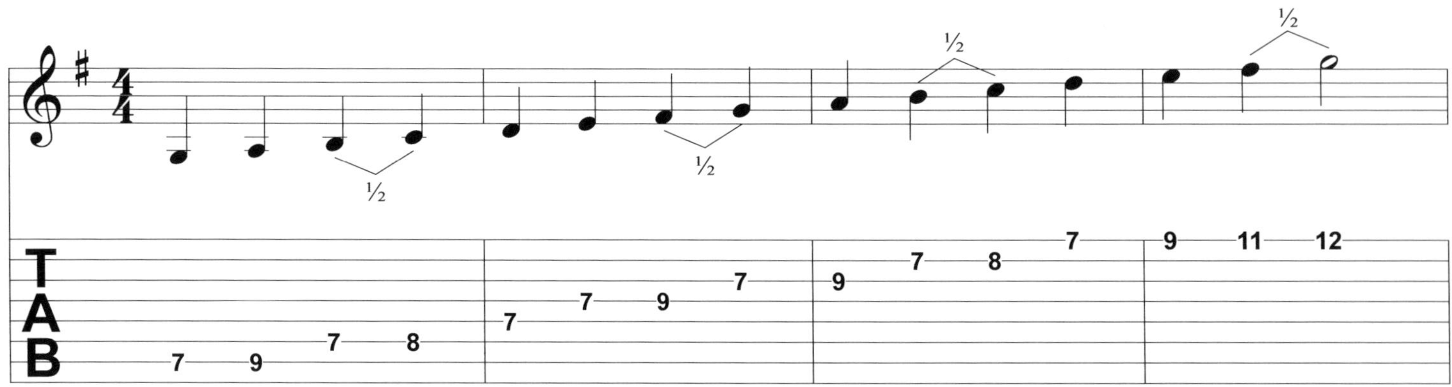

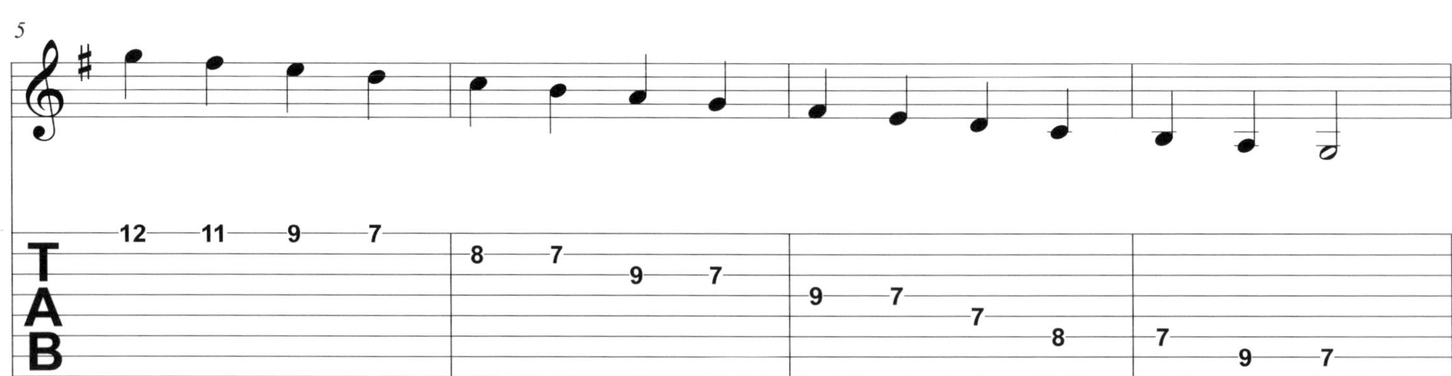

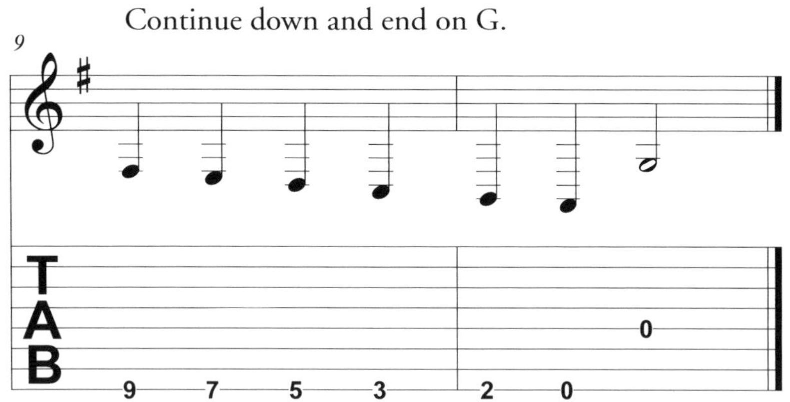

The Fender Dual 8 Professional is a popular steel guitar which was built from 1946 to 1957. It has a real "fat" tone, because of its "string-through" pickups.

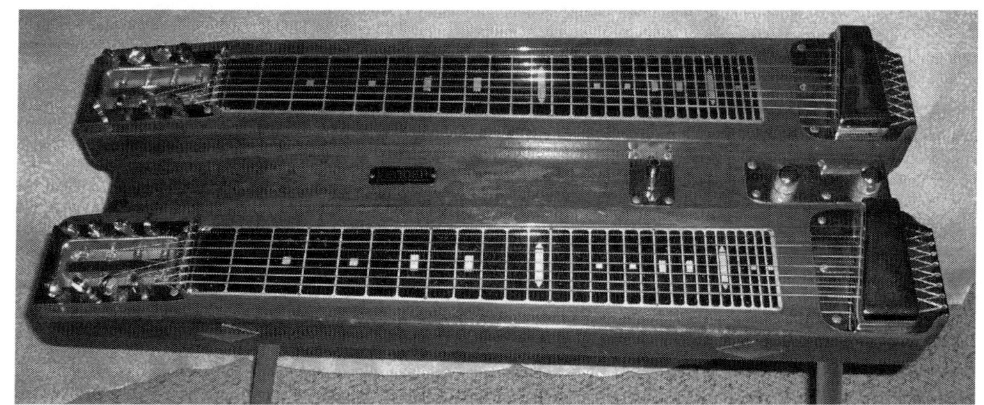

The sixth note in the G scale is E. The key of E minor is relative to the key of G. As the key signature is the same as G major, with one sharp, F♯. Beginning a scale on the 6th degree of a major scale produces the "relative minor" scale with the same key signature as its relative major scale. Note the position of the half tones between the 2nd and 3rd and 5th and 6th scale degrees. The E minor chord is also the vi minor chord in the key of G.

6

E Natural Minor Scale

The E minor scale uses the same notes as the G major scale; just start on E.

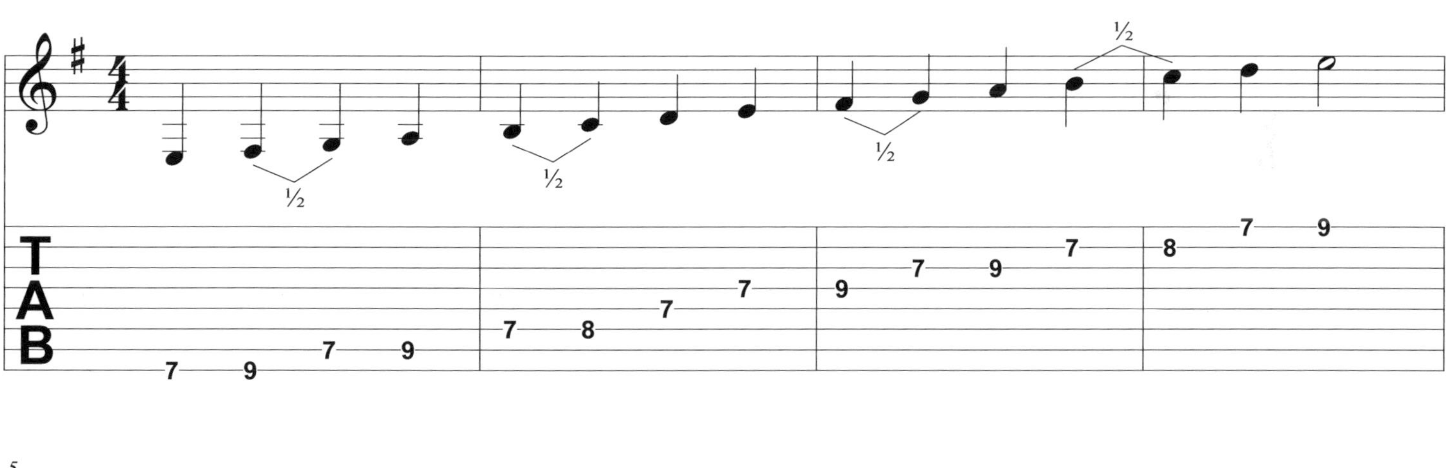

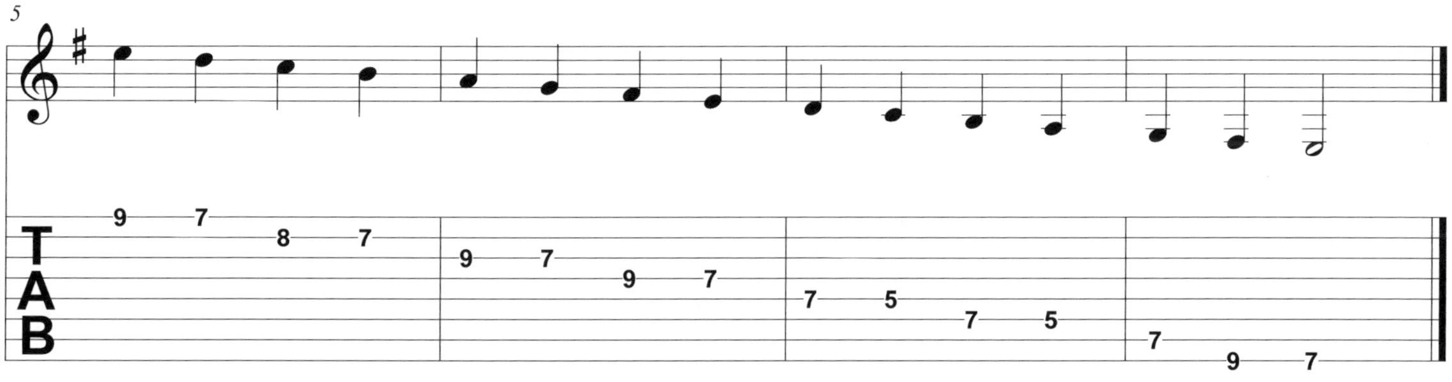

E Harmonic Minor Scale

In the E **harmonic minor** scale, the 7th note, D, is raised a half tone, so D♯ is common when playing in the key of E minor.

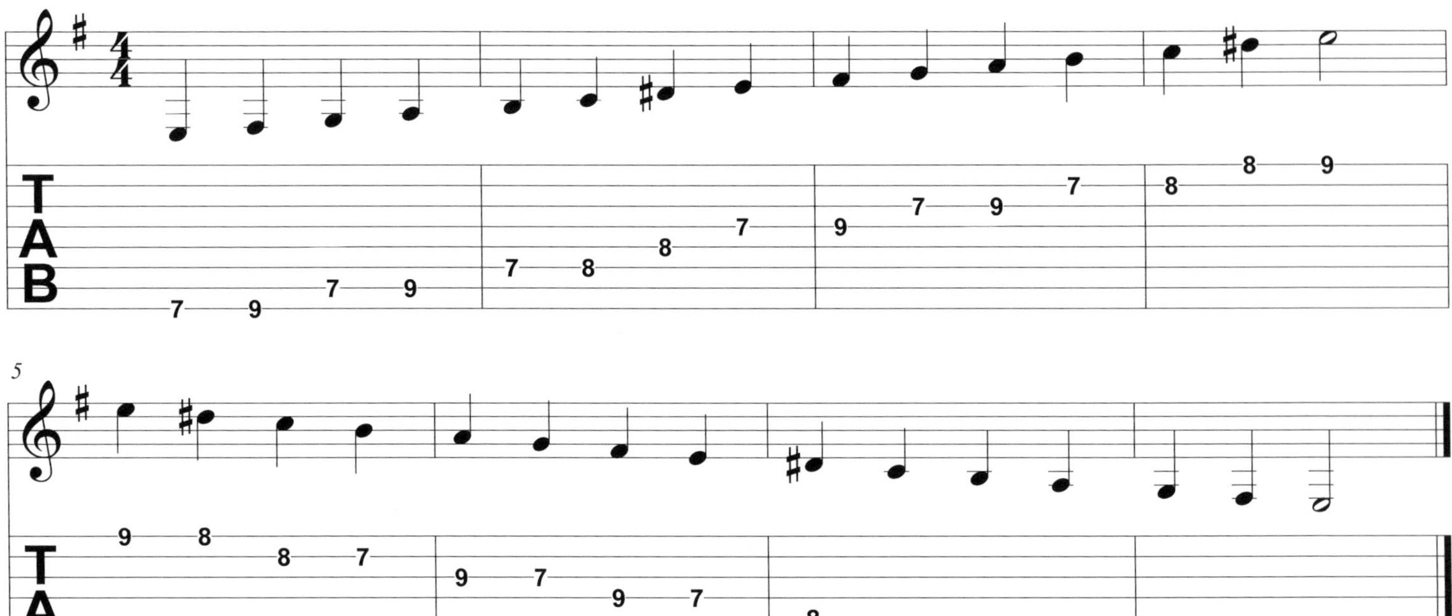

Practice these scales in the other keys listed below. Sharps and flats in the key signature are also listed. Starting at the:

2nd fret, D major and B minor	(2 sharps)
4th fret, E major and C♯ minor	(4 sharps)
5th fret, F major and D minor	(1 flat)
7th fret, G major and E minor	(1 sharp)
9th fret, A major and F♯ minor	(3 sharps)
11th fret, B major and G♯ minor	(5 sharps)

At the 12th fret, it will repeat; that is, all of the notes on the 12th fret are one octave higher than open strings/notes. An octave is defined as a tone on the eighth degree from a given tone. For example: The third string open is a C, and on the 12th fret you'll find another C an octave higher.

12th fret, C major and A minor	(no sharps or flats)
14th fret, D major and B minor	(2 sharps)
Etc.	

Note that as you go higher up the neck the distance between frets gets smaller and smaller, making it harder to play in tune.

Chord Basics

This section is going to show the basic places to play G major, G6 and Em (minor) chords or partial chords. In a lot of instances G6 is played as a substitute for G major, when it sounds appropriate. That's what gives this instrument that "swing" sound.

Here are all the G major and G⁶ chords on the 7th fret. The right-hand fingerings called "string grips" are all the same with the middle finger on the top note, index on the middle note, and thumb on the low or bottom string. The first two measures are G major, without the 6th. Note that these string grips omit the 4th and 8th strings, the E notes, to form the G major chords. The final 3 measures use identical string grips to play G⁶ chords, except for the second chord in the 3rd measure.

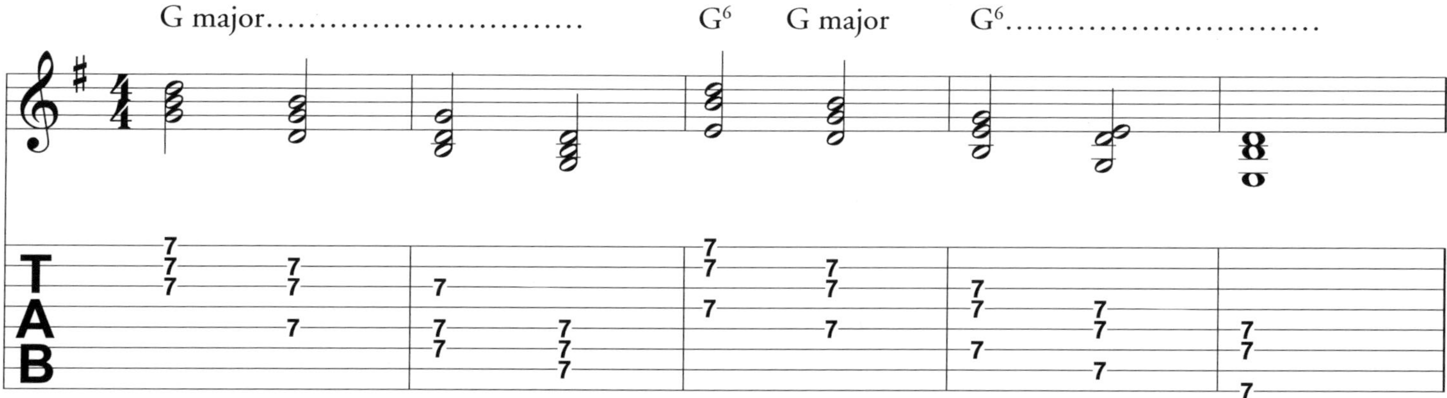

Similarly, the following G⁶ chords use the same string grips with one exception. The thumb plays the bottom two strings by picking in an upward sweeping motion. The video shows this idea in more detail.

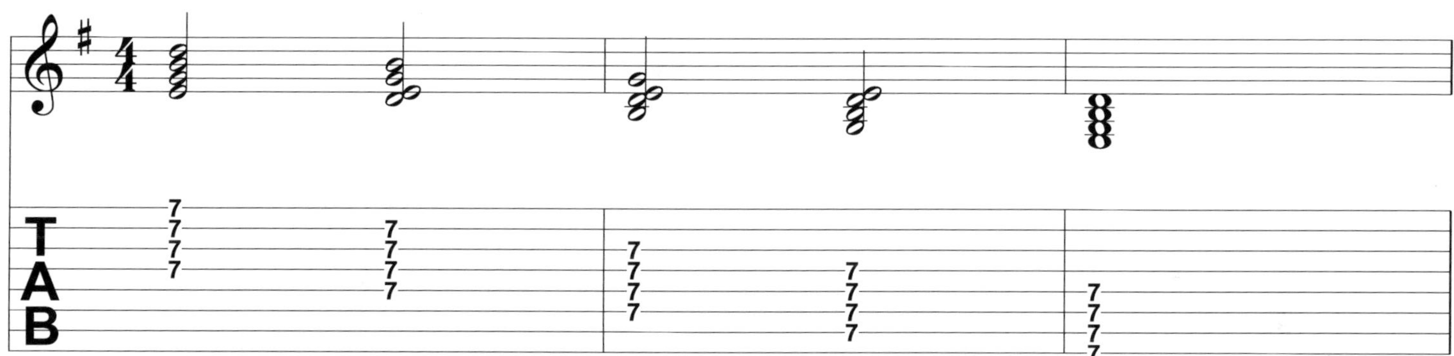

Here are G major, partial (no G note) and G⁶ two-string intervals. Technically, the simplest chord has 3 notes sounded either simultaneously or in quick succession as an arpeggio; two notes sounded together or one after the other comprise an *interval*. Right-hand fingering is done with the middle finger and thumb.

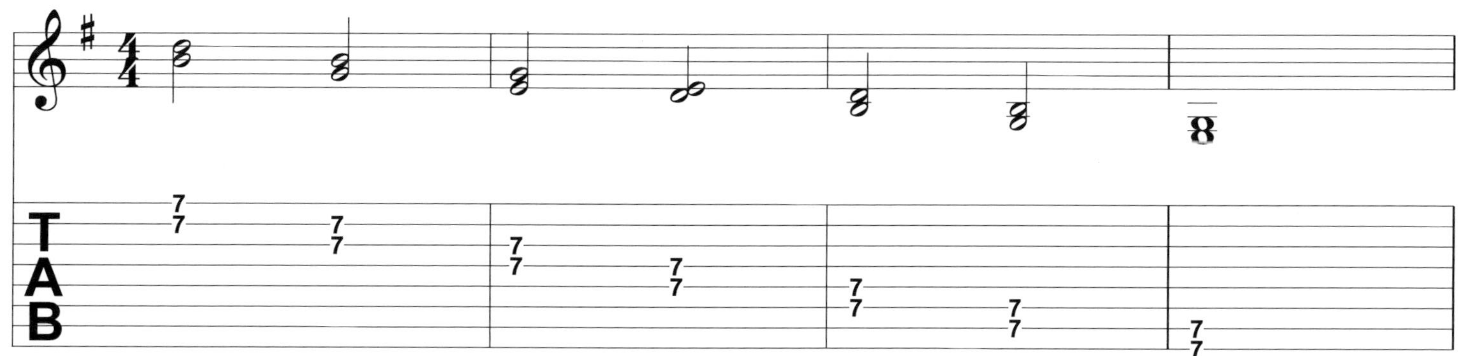

Here are a couple of common G partial chords or intervals that are not on the seventh fret.

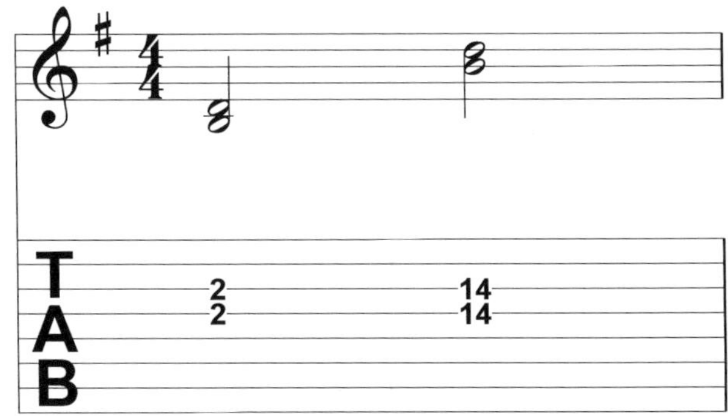

Playing Swing Eighth Notes 

Most popular music from jazz to bluegrass to country uses a "swing" feel playing eighth notes in a triplet long-short rhythm. Most classical music is not played with the swing feel, but rather as even, "straight eighths," in strict time. The music in this book is played with swing eighths unless otherwise noted. It's easier to show you with the video than to describe it in more detail.

Swing eighths can be notated in sheet music with a symbol like this:

♫ = ♩ ♪ (triplet 3)

Here are simple exercises or licks in the key of G. Note that the chord names are displayed in the first three exercises, but they all are played in the key of G, or where the band is playing a G chord. Practice these exercises at different frets in various keys. I didn't write any slide markings, but you can pick the first chord and slide up to the next chord, or pick all of the notes in each chord. Practice both ways. Swing the eighth notes. Remember, a bar line cancels the effect of accidentals in the previous measure.

Exercise 1: Use T, M, I (thumb, middle, index on the right hand)

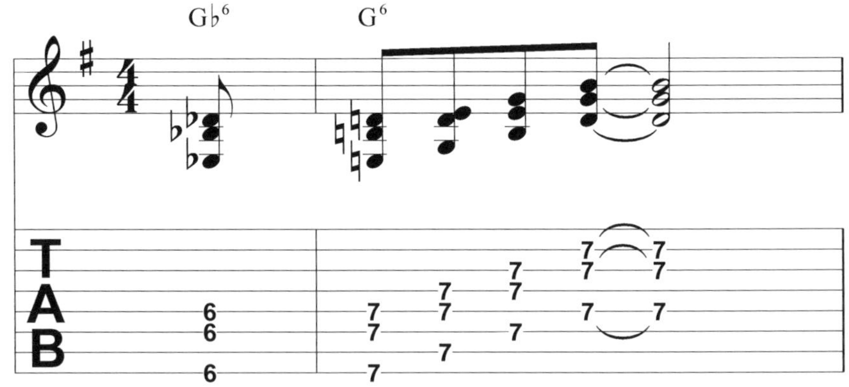

Exercise 2: Use T and M

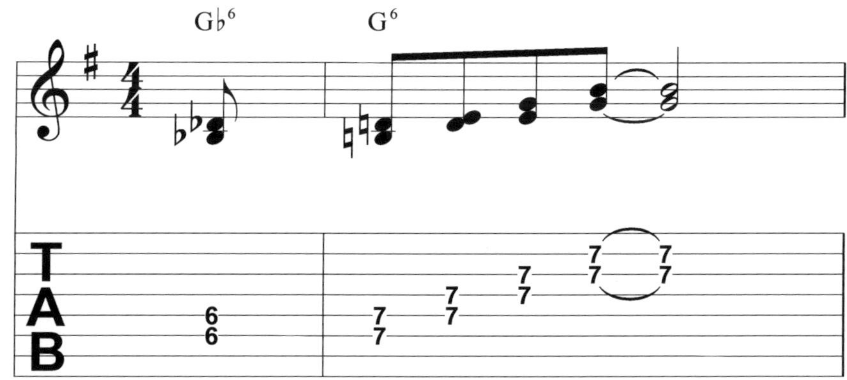

Exercise 3: Use T, M, I

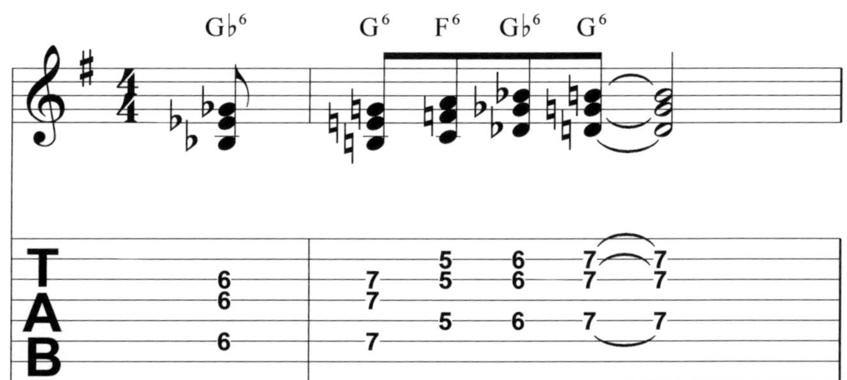

Exercise 4: Use T and M. This lick works well as an ending.

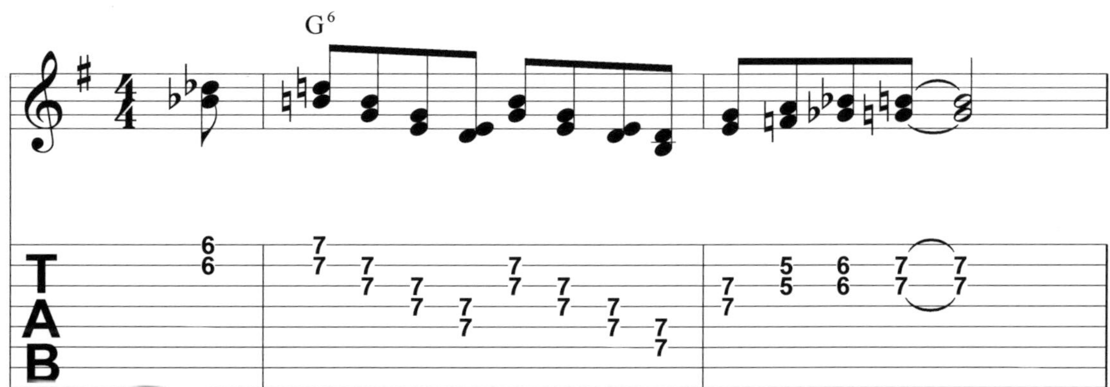

When a non-pedal steel guitar has multiple necks and legs, it is referred to as a "console." The Gibson Console Grande is a beautiful guitar popularized by Don Helms, the steel guitar player with Hank Williams' Drifting Cowboys. Don also played on Hank's recordings.

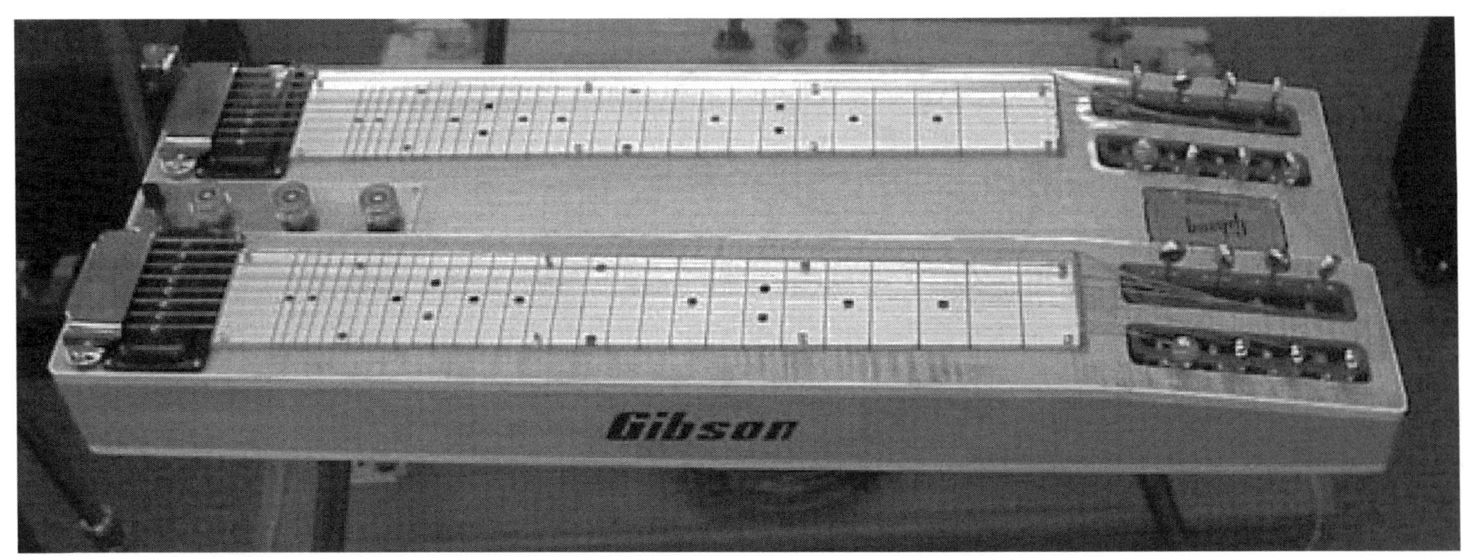

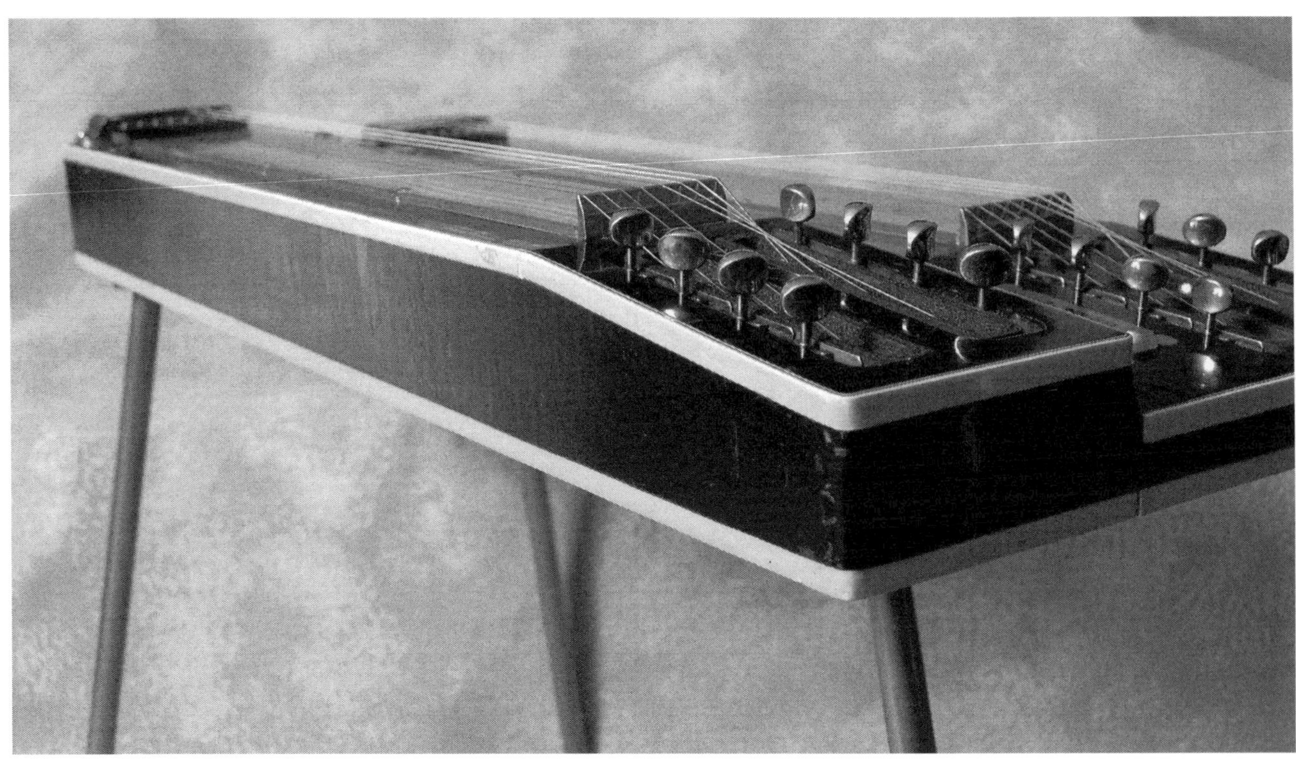

Joyful, Joyful (Ode to Joy) in the key of G

I once got a lucrative wedding gig because I can read music in standard notation. Most steel players cannot read music. This song is simple. Note that the piece includes a chord with a slash and another letter; this symbol represents a chord with a note other than the tonic in the bass. It doesn't mean anything to you as a steel player, but if you gave this chart to a bass player, the second letter is what the bass plays. For example, G/D is a G chord with a D in the bass.

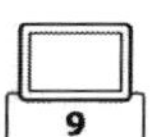

Joyful, Joyful (Ode to Joy) in G

Ludwig van Beethoven

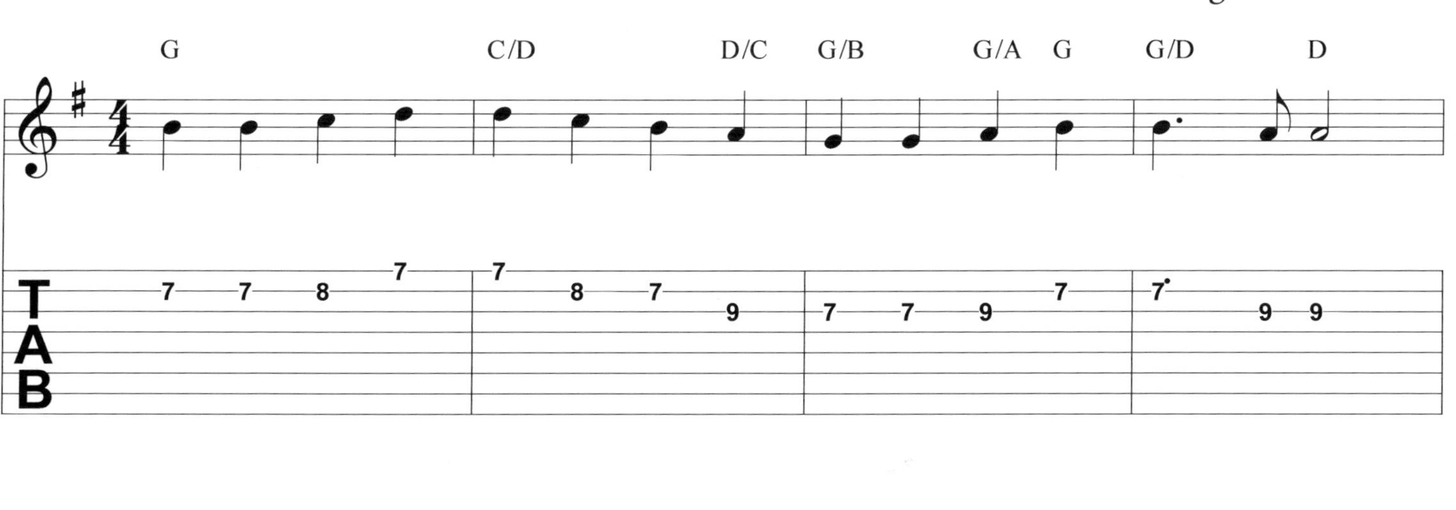

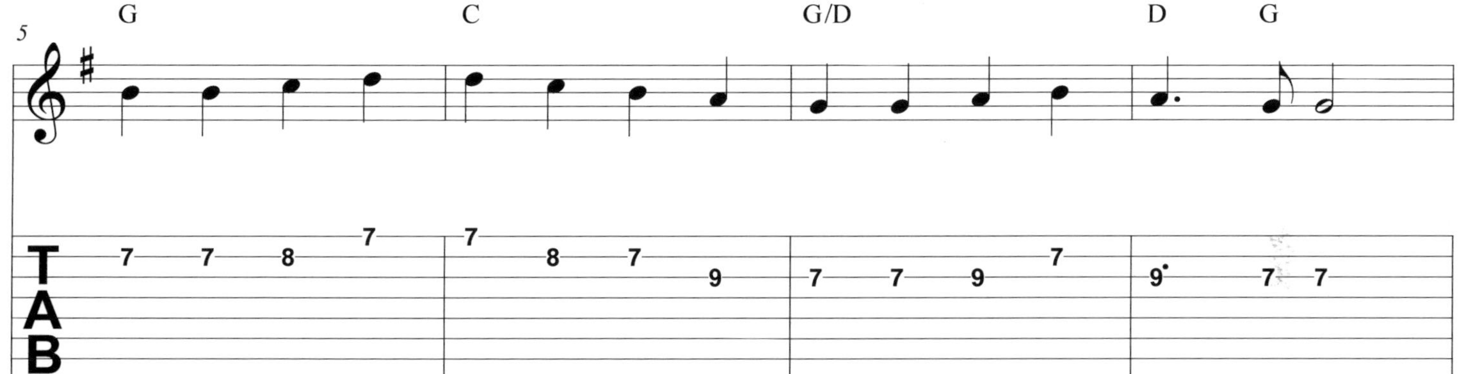

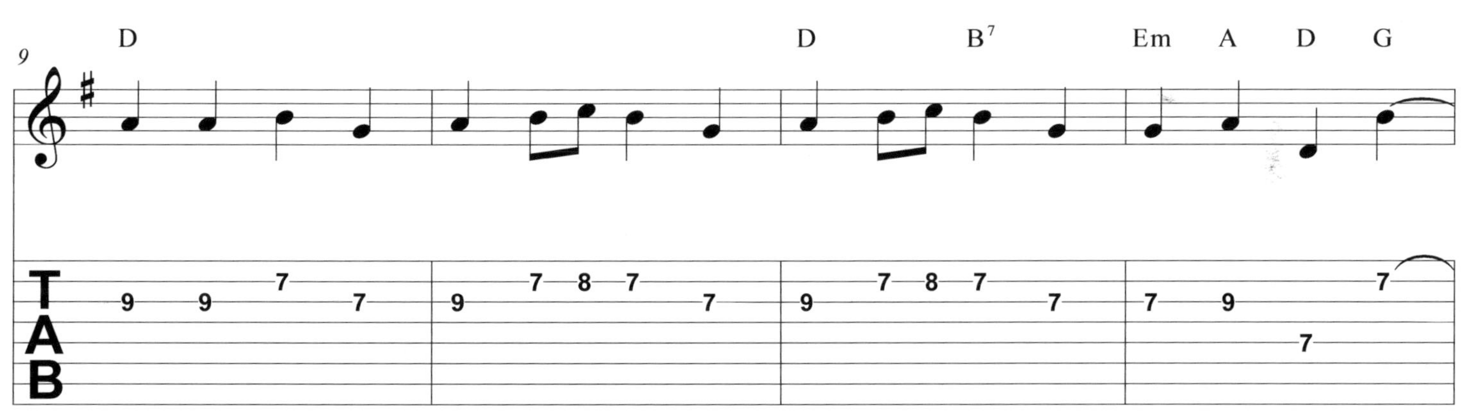

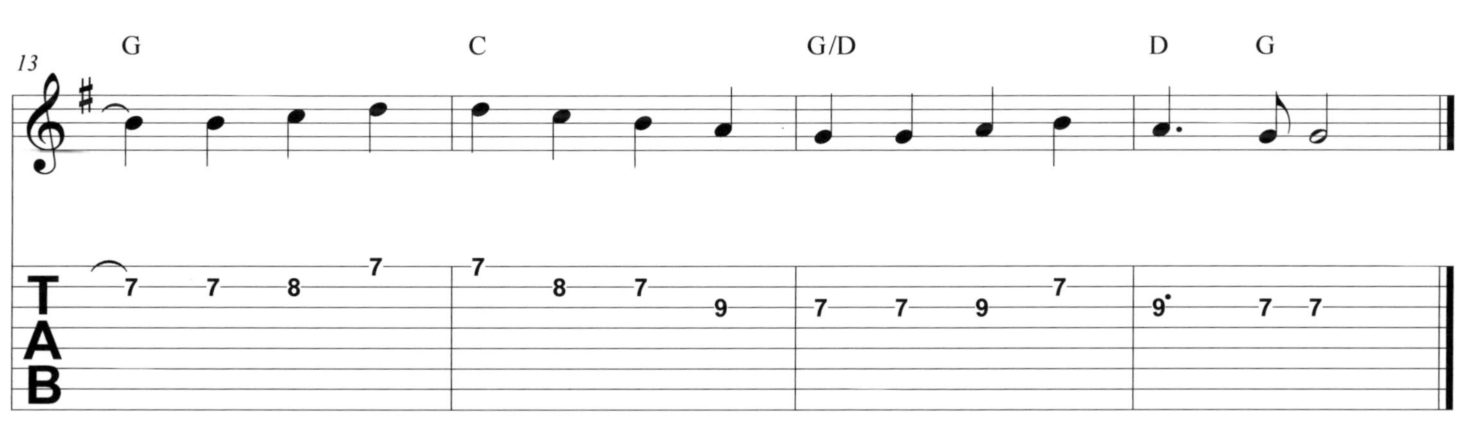

Joyful, Joyful (Ode to Joy) in the key of C

Practice playing this song in different keys. Because it's in "closed" position, meaning there are no open strings, it's easy to play it the same way at a different fret. Move up to the 12th fret to play it in C, then try it in D, E, F, A, and B.

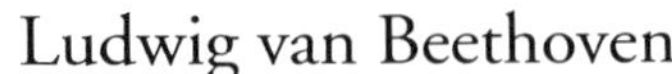
Ludwig van Beethoven

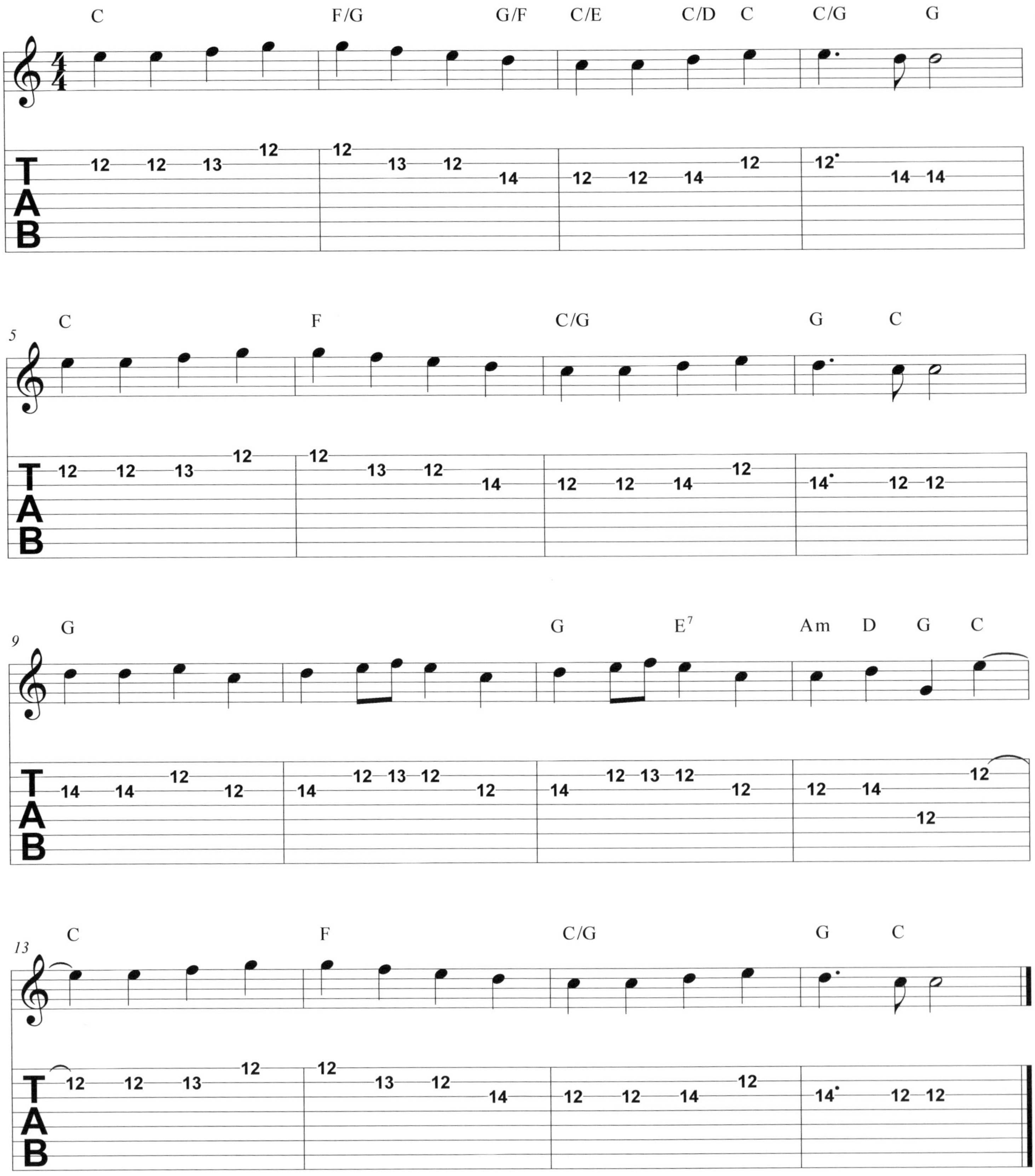

Joyful, Joyful (Ode to Joy) in the key of C, down an octave

Here is the song down an octave in the first position using open strings. Practice playing the notes in tune. Note the eighth and half-note Cs in measures 8 and 16. You could slide up to the noted C half note and play two C's in unison on two adjacent strings.

Ludwig van Beethoven

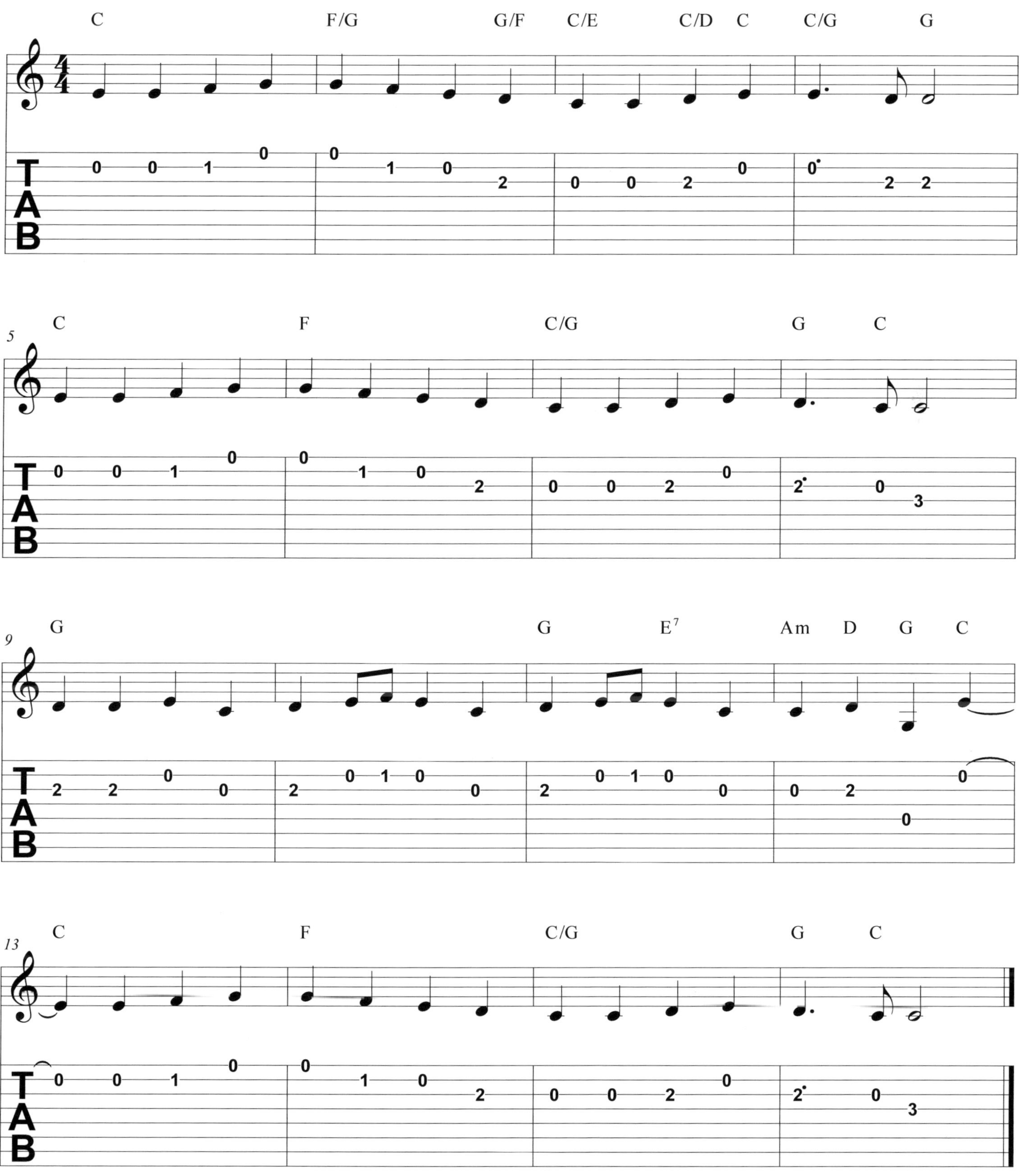

There are some Dobros® or resophonic guitars that have 7 or 8 strings like this Sho-Bro. You can add the 6th to the extra string and tune it like a C6 non-pedal steel guitar. Think of it as an acoustic non-pedal steel guitar. You can play it not only as a traditional Dobro®, with Stevens-style bar, but as a steel guitar using "bullet" bar and steel guitar right-hand blocking.

This guitar was made by Shot Jackson of the Sho-Bud Steel Guitar Company in Nashville in 1973. Apparently, when Shot started making the guitars after Gretsch in 1973; he would buy guitar bodies from Harmony Sovereign and make his bodies from these. Shot made the necks and a guy who had a shop around the corner on Broadway did the inlays.

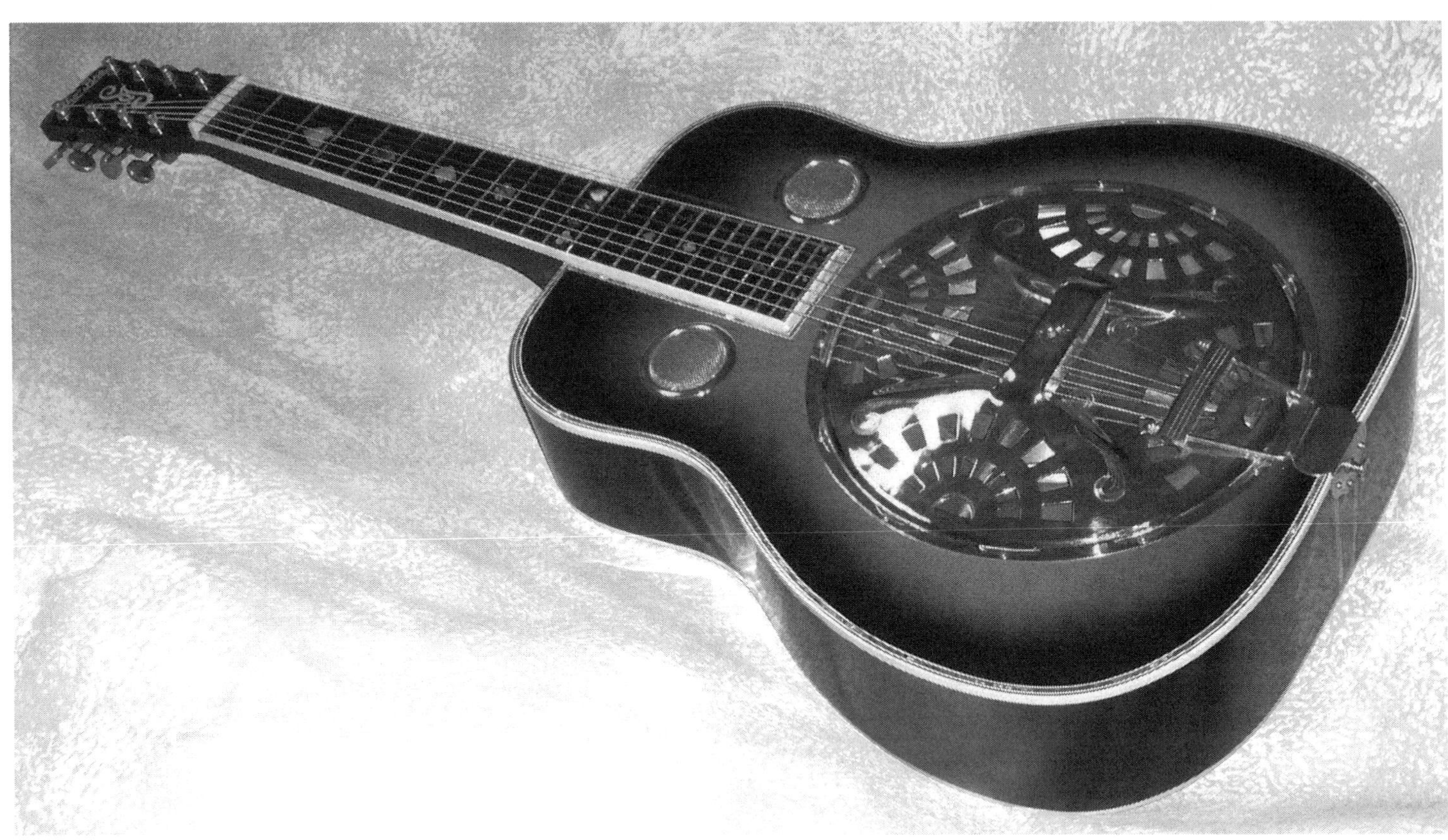

Don Helms-Style Intro and Outro

In the following music notation there are some items that you might not have seen before. *Ritard* means the tempo gradually slows down. A dotted note is a note with a small dot written after it. The dot increases the duration of the note by half of the note's original value. For instance a dotted half note, gets 3 beats. A dotted quarter note, gets 1 ½ beats. A tie is drawn as an arc-shaped line connecting two notes of the same pitch. The pair of tied notes acts as one note with their time values added together.

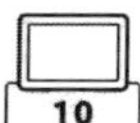

Don Helms-Style Intro

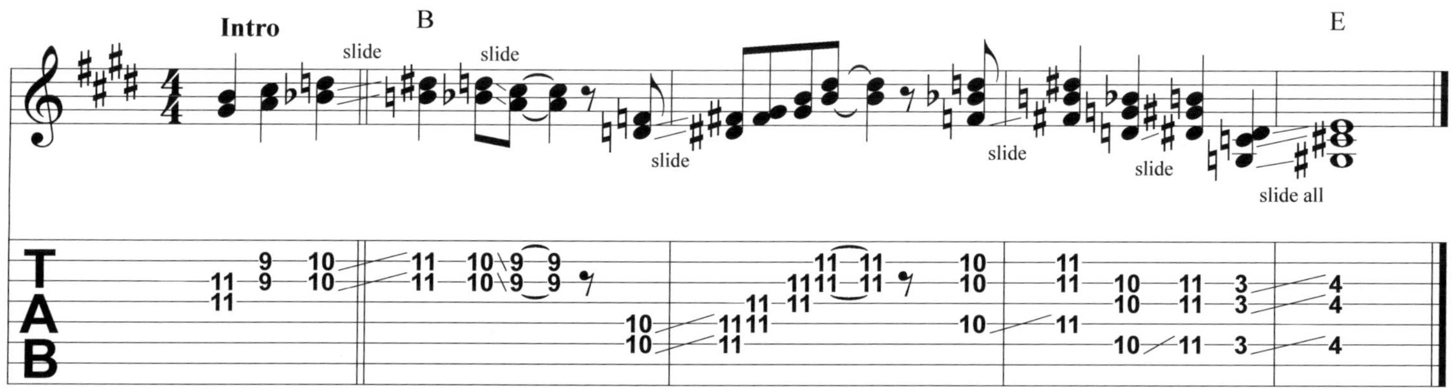

Don Helms-Style Outro

The right hand is all T (thumb) and M (middle) except the last chord. That's a rake across the string with the thumb and slide up to the E6 chord.

The notes before the slide are picked and then slid up or down.

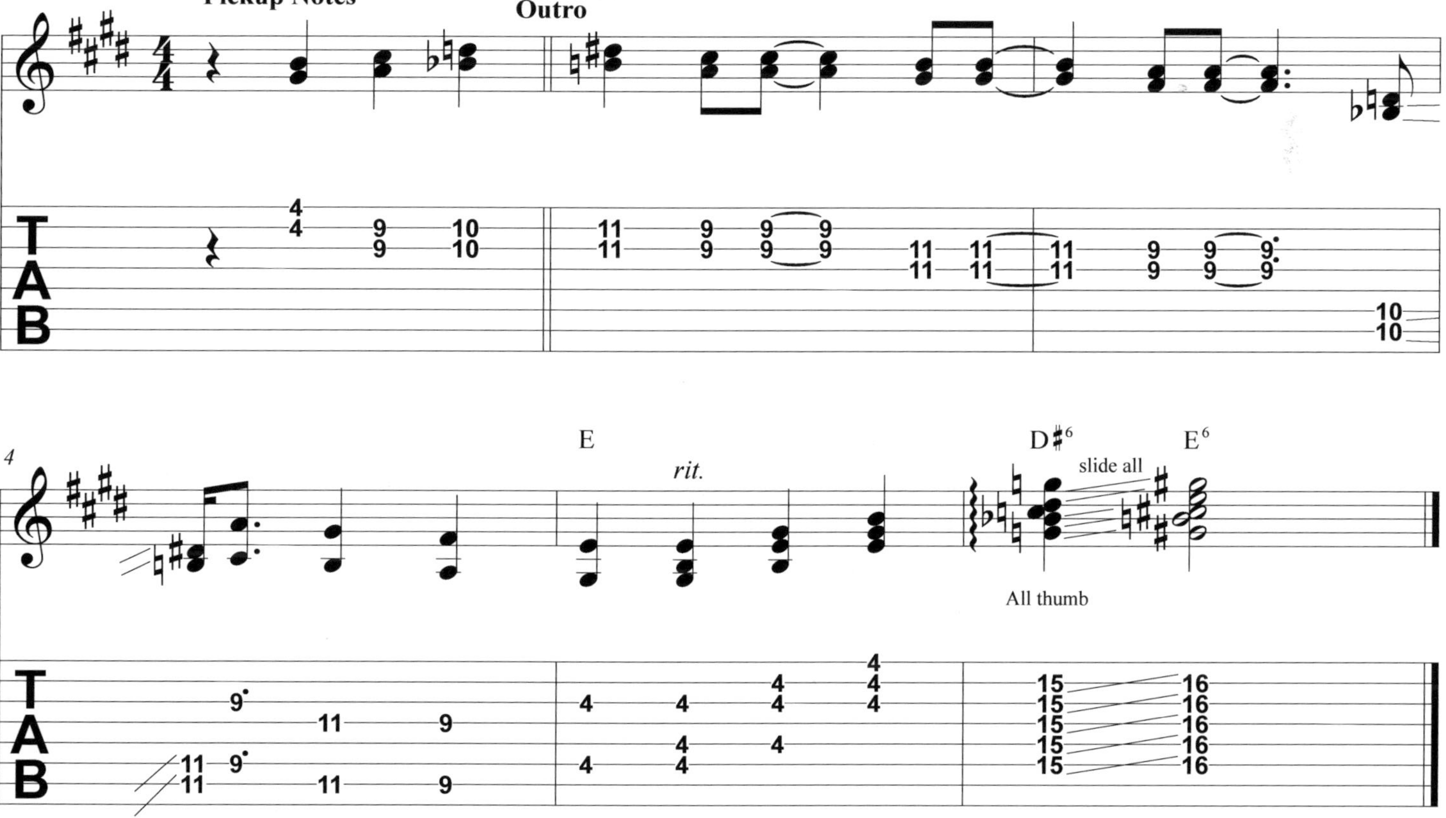

The Nashville Number System

The Nashville Number System is a method of writing the chords to a song using numbers instead of chord names. This way the song can be played in any key at any time without rewriting it.

The basic principle in writing charts is that each letter is one measure of music. The premise behind the Nashville Number System is simple. Instead of using the chord names in a chart:

C F G C

We use numbers. The numbers are correlated to the scale. In the key of C,

	C	D	E	F	G	A	B	C
becomes:	1	2	3	4	5	6	7	1

A song with a C, F, and G chord progression would look like this:

1 4 5 1

The advantage of using number charts is that one chart is valid for all key signatures. If the singer informs the leader or producer, *"The key of C is too high for me. Can we try it B♭?"* Sure, no need to re-write the chart. 1, 4, 5, 1 in the key of B♭ would translate to:

B♭ E♭ F B♭

For more information on the Nashville Number System visit my website:
www.robhainesstudio.com/numchart

On the website there is a section on Chart Basics that show you how to get started and a place to obtain the custom fonts used in making charts on a computer.

The following is a simple number chart. The ||: and :|| characters mean that you repeat the main body of the chart, the verse and chorus sections, as needed.

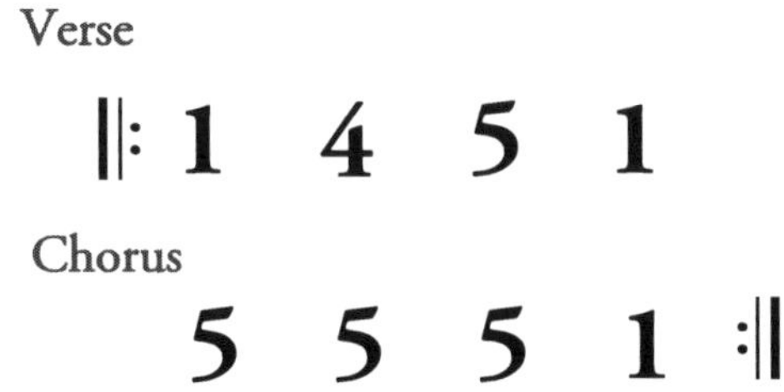

Don Helms-Style Intro and Outro Nashville Number Chart

Key of E

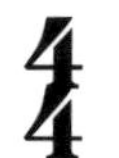 (four beats per measure; a quarter note gets one beat)

Intro **5 5 5 1**

Outro **5 5 5 1 1^6**

Right-Hand Technique, Alternating Thumb/Middle 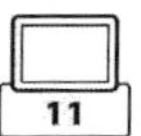

The thumb picks down and the middle picks up. Use a metronome to assure timing and accuracy. Start slow and gradually pick up speed as the middle finger is stronger than the index, you would normally use the middle finger with this type of picking, but practice using the index with the thumb as a way of building its strength. The next step is to invent your own picking exercises, alternating thumb/middle patterns. Use different strings and the bar to go up the neck.

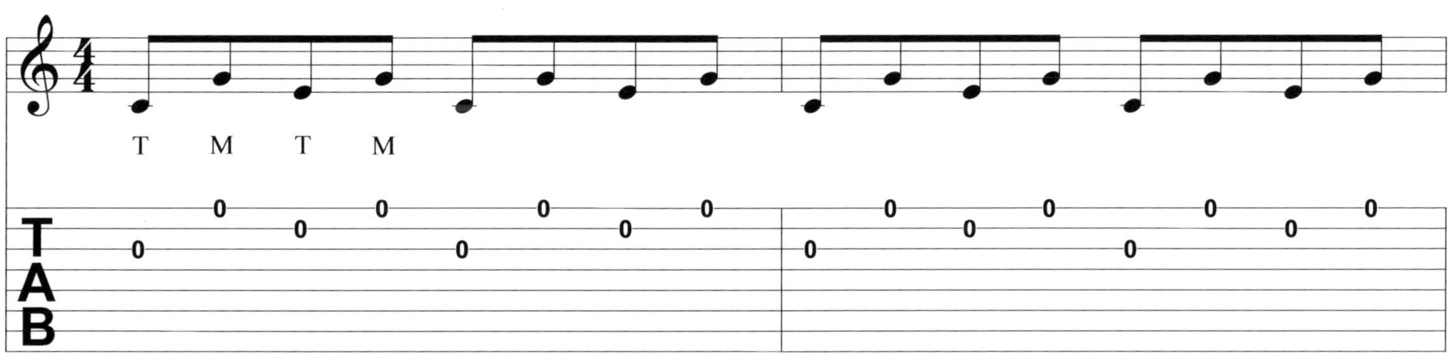

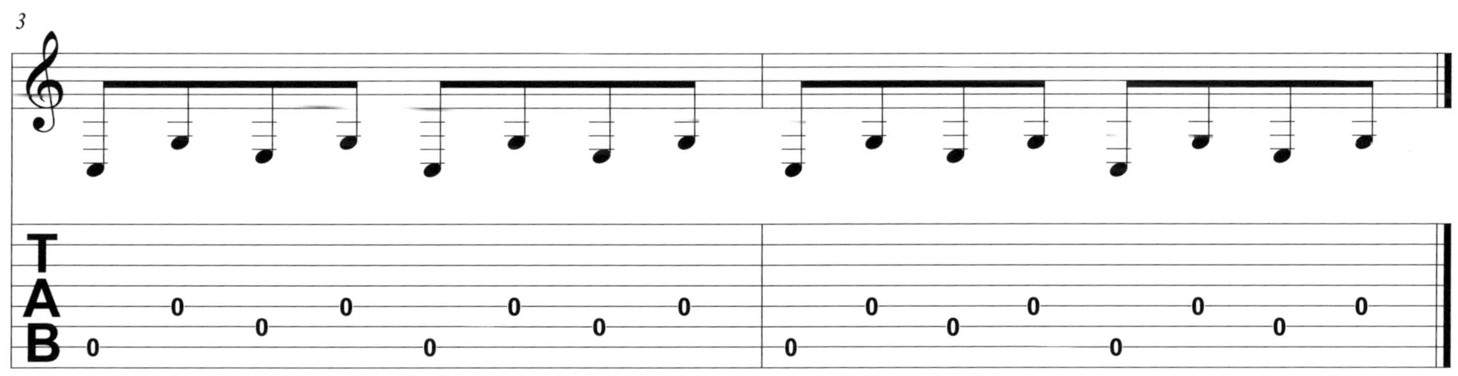

Now familiarize yourself with the notes of the C scale on the 7th string. Go up and down the string just learning the notes, what fret they are on and what they sound like. The first two measures are in C major and the next two measures are C minor. The right-hand fingering is not important.

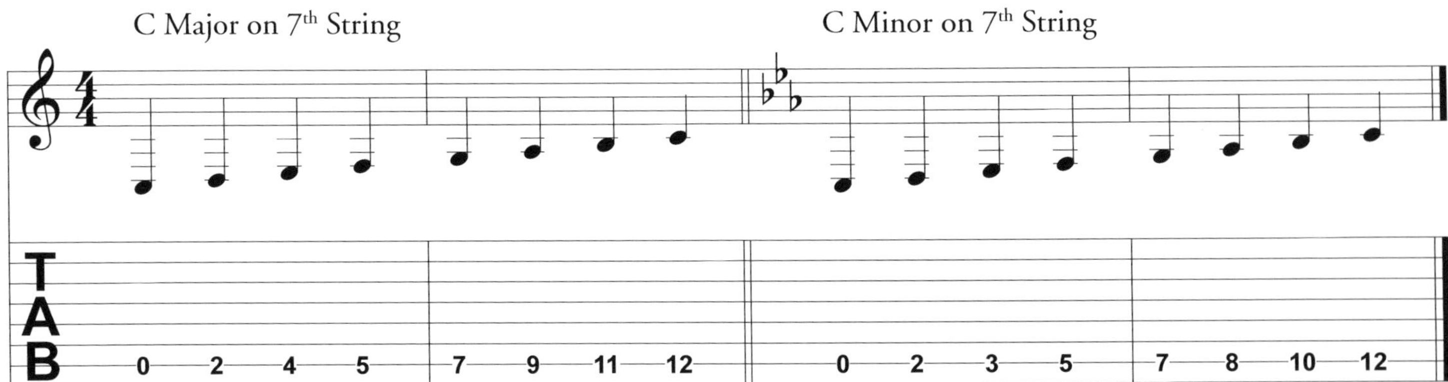

This next exercise uses some notes from the C minor scale. Keep the fingering as the thumb on the 7th string and middle on the 5th string. Practice slow and fast, with a metronome.

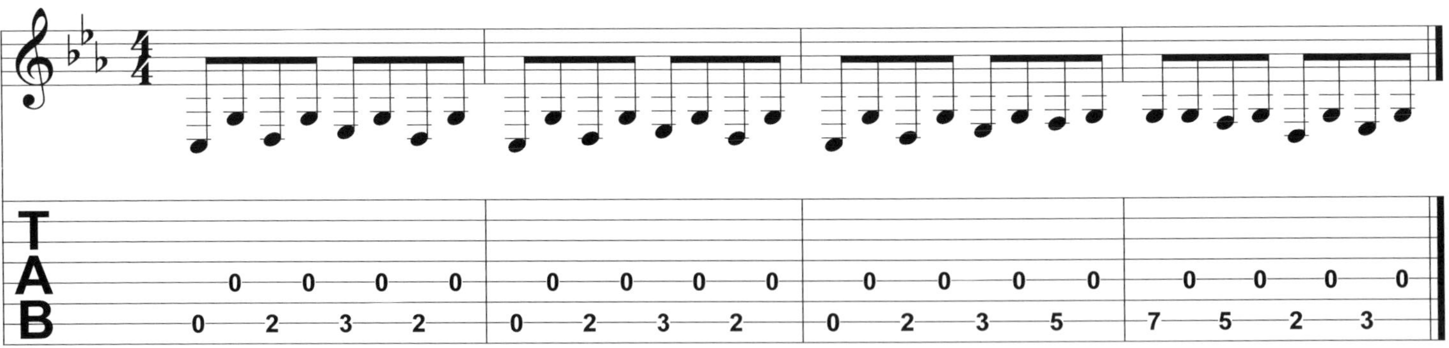

Then create your own exercises or just "noodle" around. Experiment with different notes on the 7th string; don't be afraid of hitting a bad note. It's good "ear training" to learn what sounds good and what sounds bad. Also, don't stick with just the notes in the scales. Try everything and anything.

Try including some accidental notes. An accidental is a note that is not a member of the scale in the key of the piece. For instance, hitting an E♭ before an E, or a B before a C in the key of C major creates tension that is resolved on the note after the accidental. It also sounds great.

The next exercise is a little more challenging because you are alternating the fingering across the strings. As with the previous exercise, use a metronome to increase speed and finger strength. The music below is in the key of D with the bar at the second fret. Practice this exercise in different keys, at different frets and even in open position.

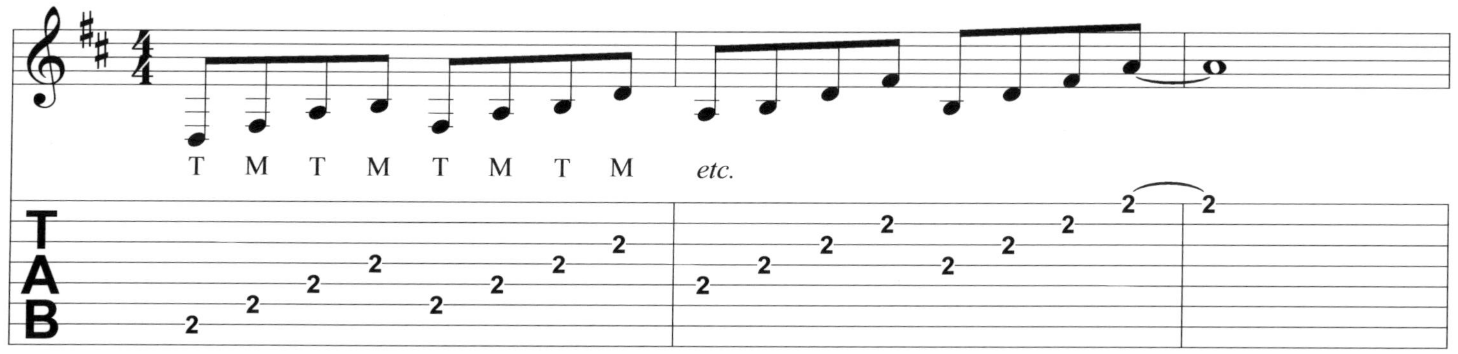

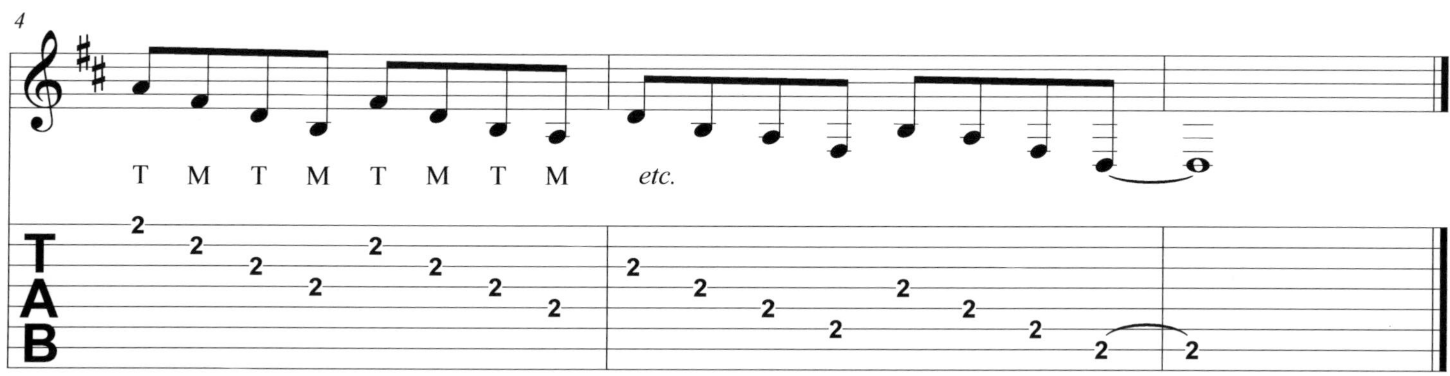

Lick Using Alternating Thumb/Middle

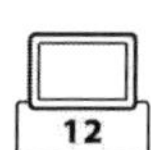

Actually, this is a combination of two licks that can be put together as one. Hit the first note, slide up one fret. At the third string, hit the note and slide down one fret.

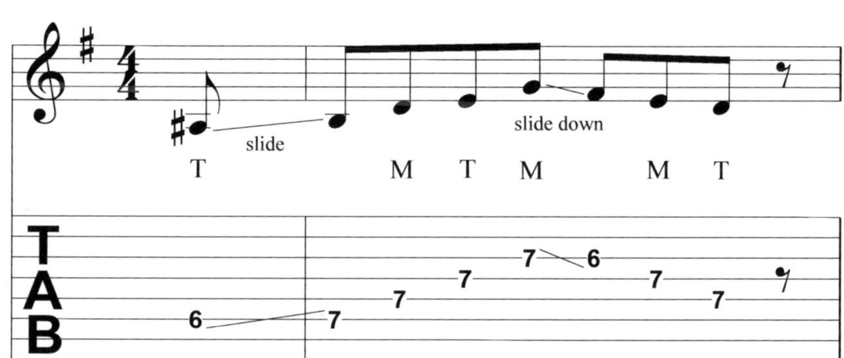

Here's the second half. Make sure you move the bar back to the 7th fret immediately after hitting the first note and all the F natural notes.

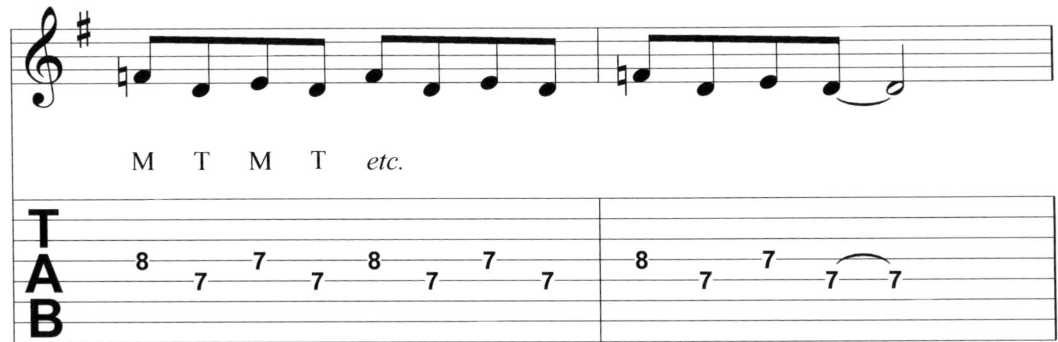

Now put the licks together.

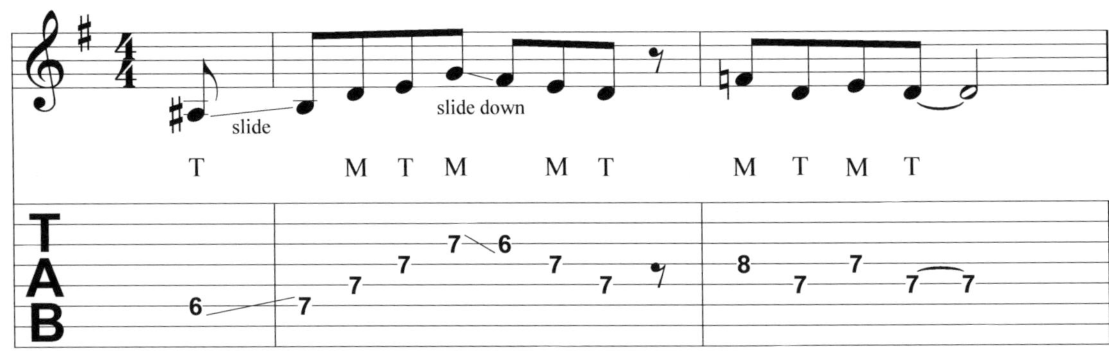

Here's a different way to do the second lick. Even though the tab says 8th fret, keep the bar on the 7th fret and pull the fourth string to get the F-natural note. Practice these licks in different keys and different tempos.

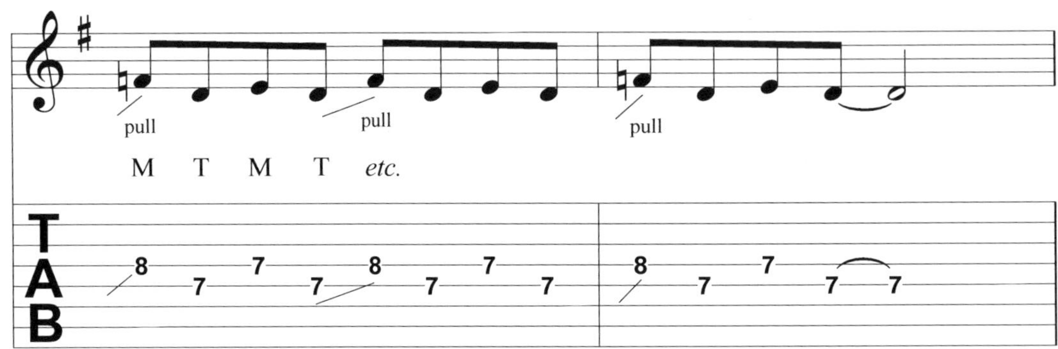

Chromatic Lick

Here's a chromatic-sounding lick using the thumb and middle fingers of the right hand. For most people, the middle finger is stronger than the index. So call it a "speed lick" using the thumb and middle. Start slow and build up speed. It helps to practice this and all other licks with a metronome. Then, call it an exercise and use the index finger with the thumb to build up strength in the index. It's written out in A and C, but should be practiced in many different keys.

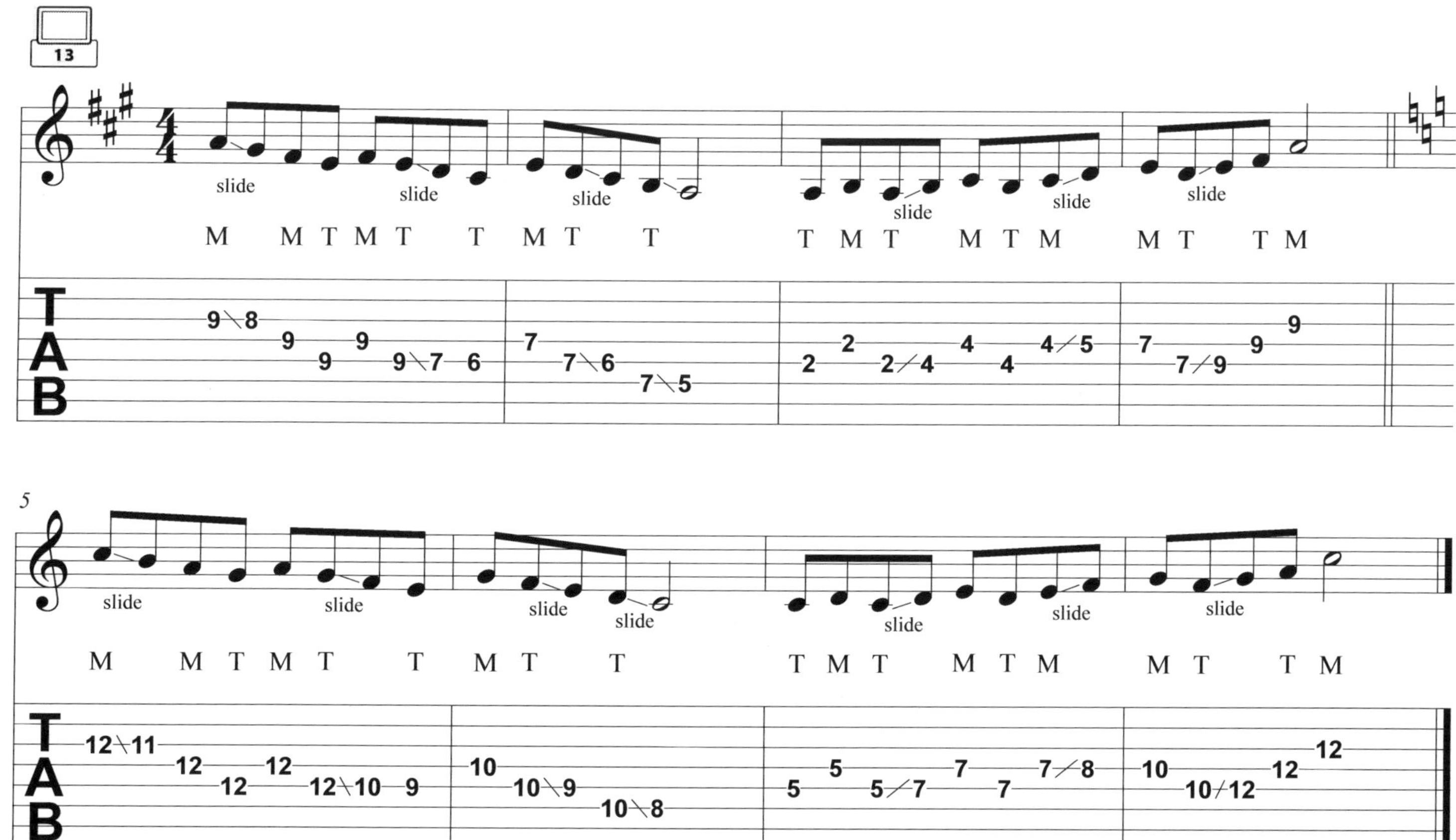

It's hard to find vintage 10-string, non-pedal steel guitars. The Eddie Alkire Eharp was the most harmonically advanced single-neck lap steel guitar available when it was designed around 1940. Alkire was a well-know Hawaiian guitarist and early pioneer of the 10-string steel who ran a teaching studio. These instruments were primarily sold to his advanced students. Although made by Epiphone, they carry only the "Alkire Eharp" nameplate.

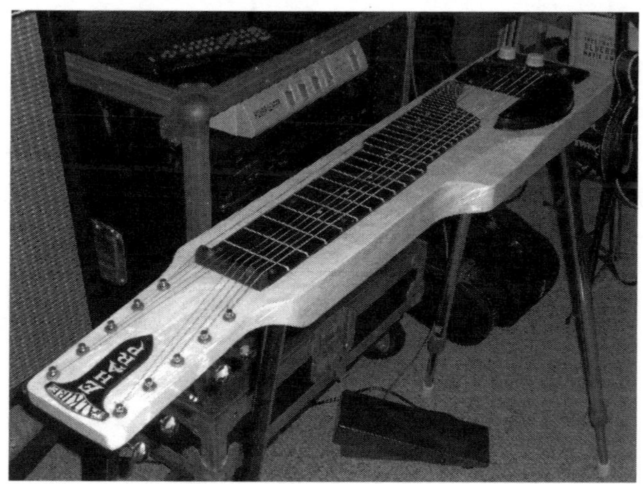

5 5 5 1 Intro

In a lot of types of music there are generic intros that can be used with many songs in any key. The following intro uses a chord progression of "5 5 5 1." That is three measures of 5 resolving to the "1" chord. The last half of the 1 chord and the last measure is optional as a filler lick. This example is written in the key of G, but it works in any key. Practice it in many keys by moving the fret positions. For instance, move everything up two frets (higher) and it becomes 5 5 5 1 in the key of A. Move it down 3 frets and it becomes the key of E.

Note that the "filler" lick at the end only works in G, because of the open first string. This lick has a major seventh sound because the G♭ or F♯ on the second string is the major seventh of a G scale. It's a nice sound having the G and G♭ ring together an octave apart.

In a live band situation you can count "one, two", play the two pickup notes (on 3 and 4) and this establishes the tempo for the rest of the band.

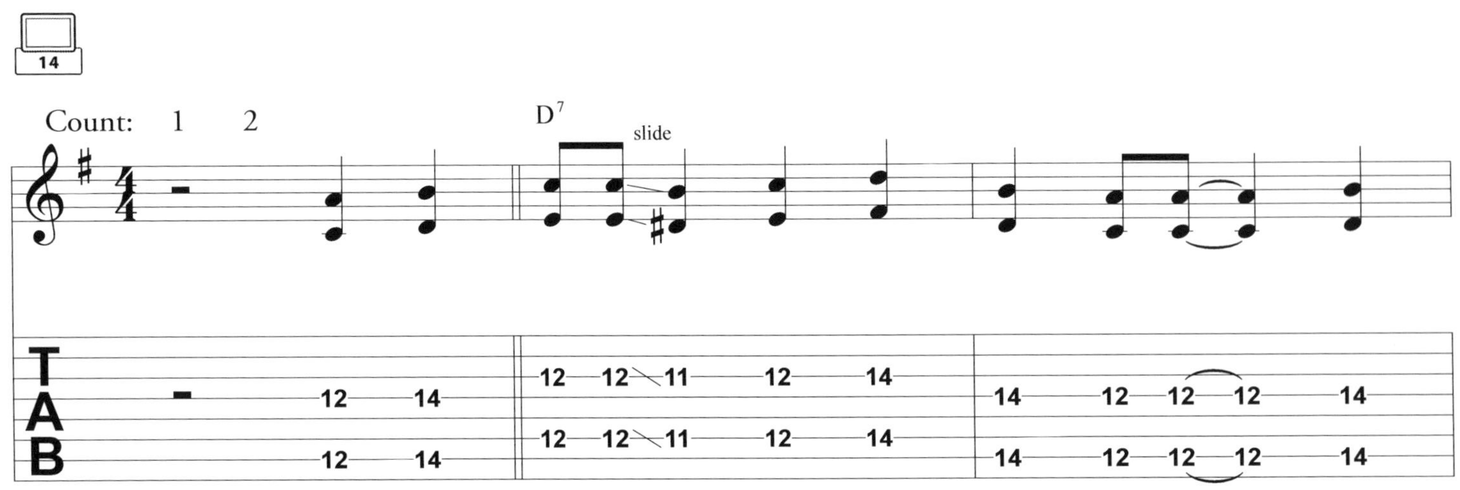

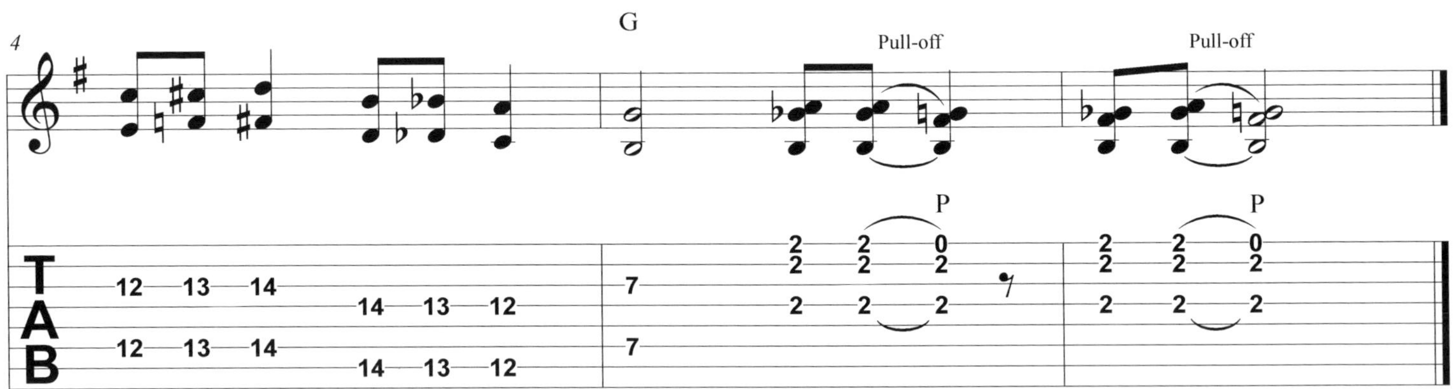

Here is the Nashville Number chart without the last filler lick.

Intro **5^7 5^7 5^7 1**

Yodel Lick

This is a very common lick that sounds like a Jimmie Rodgers yodel. It can be used as an introduction, turnaround or ending. Use the thumb on the bottom strings and middle on the top ones. If you use it as an intro, use the count-off. Assuming that there is an extra measure of G after what is written, you could call it a *1/5 11* into. Practice this in a lot of different keys.

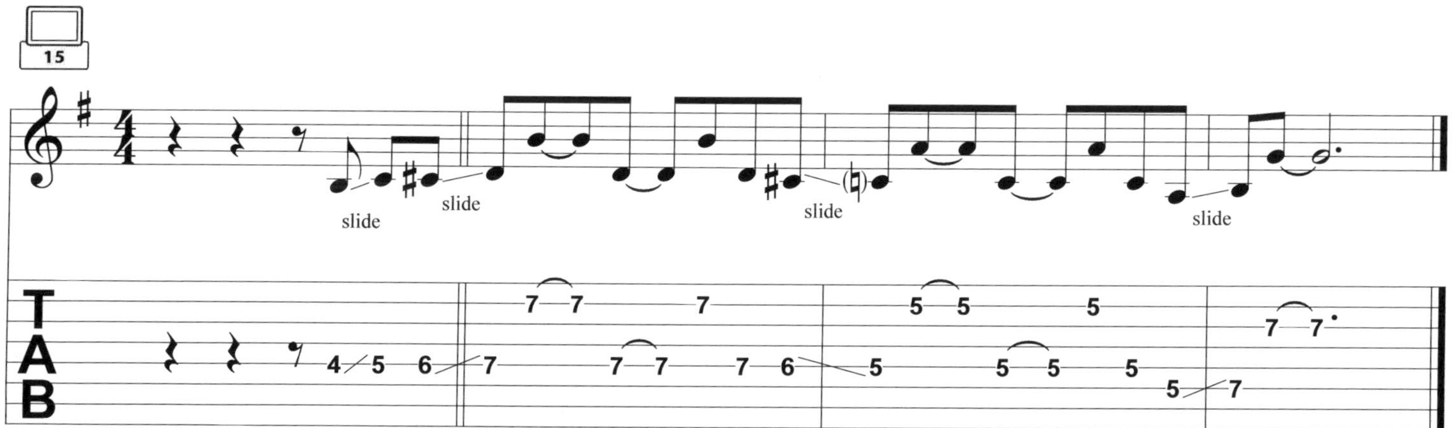

Natural Harmonics

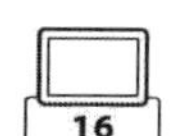

Natural harmonics occur on the open strings at the 5th, 7th and 12th frets. Start with the harmonics on the 12th fret. With the left hand, lightly touch a string at the 12th fret and, with the thumb of the right hand, pick the string. If you pick the third string it's a C note, an octave higher than the open string. Practice picking these harmonics and realize you have to just barely touch the string with the left hand over the fret to get the best sound. The harmonics at the 5th fret are an octave higher than at the 12th fret. The harmonics at the 7th fret are a fifth from the open note. So the harmonic on the 7th fret of the third string is a G note. G is the fifth in the key of C.

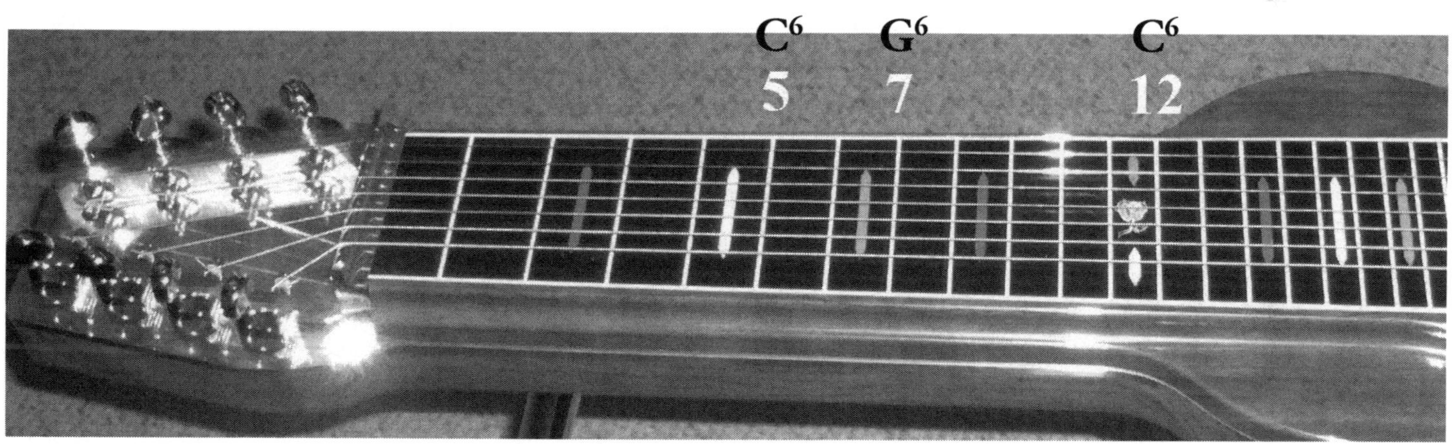

You can use the ring finger of the left hand to make chords by barring across multiple strings. In standard notation and tablature, harmonics are often depicted as follows:

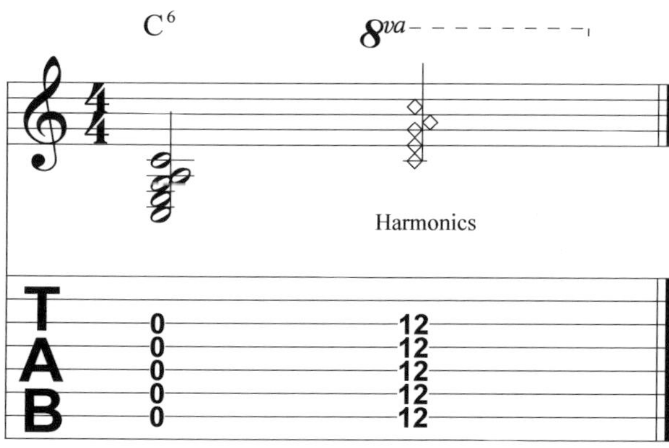

Tuning with Natural Harmonics

1. Tune the 3rd string (C) to an electronic tuner.
2. Match the 1st string harmonic at the 12th fret (G) to the 3rd string harmonic at the 7th fret (G).
3. Play the open 2nd (E) and third (C) strings together and make the 2nd string slightly flat, until the "beating" or "pulsing" goes away. Don't change string 3 as it is tuned to the tuner.
4. Match the 4th string (A) harmonic at the 7th fret (E) to the 2nd string harmonic at the 12th fret (E).
5. Tune the 5th string (low G) harmonic at the 12th fret to the open string 1 (G).
6. Tune the 6th string (low E) harmonic at the 12th fret to the open string 2 (E).
7. Tune the 7th string (low C) harmonic at the 12th fret to the open string 3 (C).
8. Tune the 8th string (low A) harmonic at the 12th fret to the open string 4 (A).

Note that the lower four strings are all tuned with 12th-fret harmonics matching their octave counterparts on the top four strings. Consequently, it's very important to tune the first four strings accurately, and then using octave harmonics, tune the low strings to match the high strings.

The Forward-Bar Slant (F-Slant) 

The front of the bar is on a higher fret than the back of the bar. Practice the exercise below as written and with different frets/chords. Note, the higher you go up the fretboard, the less the bar is slanted and the harder it is to play in tune. The video goes into more detail on left-hand technique for bar slants. Slant the bar with the hand while keeping your left arm straight.

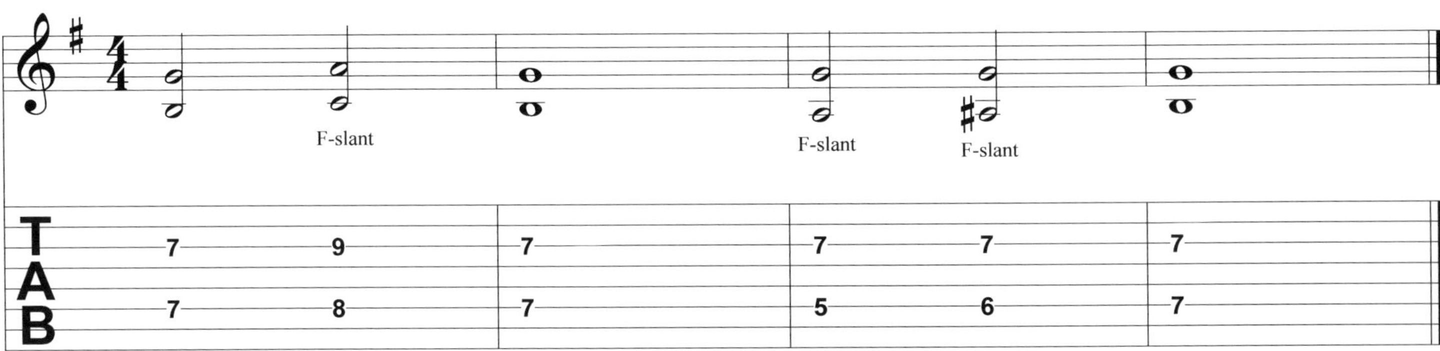

Here's a G scale with the harmony note on the bottom. Practice this scale in all keys. Work on playing in time and most importantly, in tune.

It takes a lot of practice to slant the bar without thinking about what you are doing. It's called "muscle memory." When you do the same thing over and over again, it gets easier over time. You start to do it without thinking. That's muscle memory.

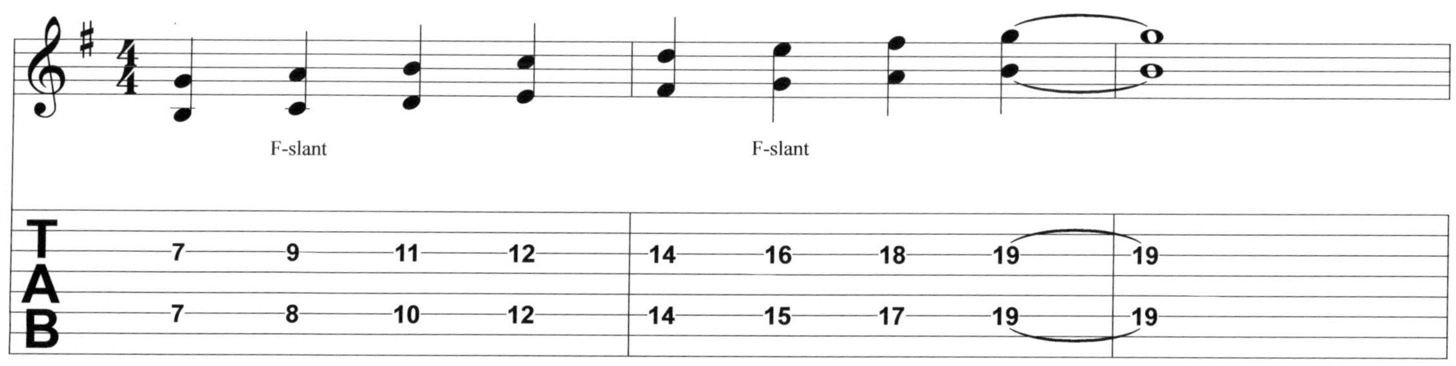

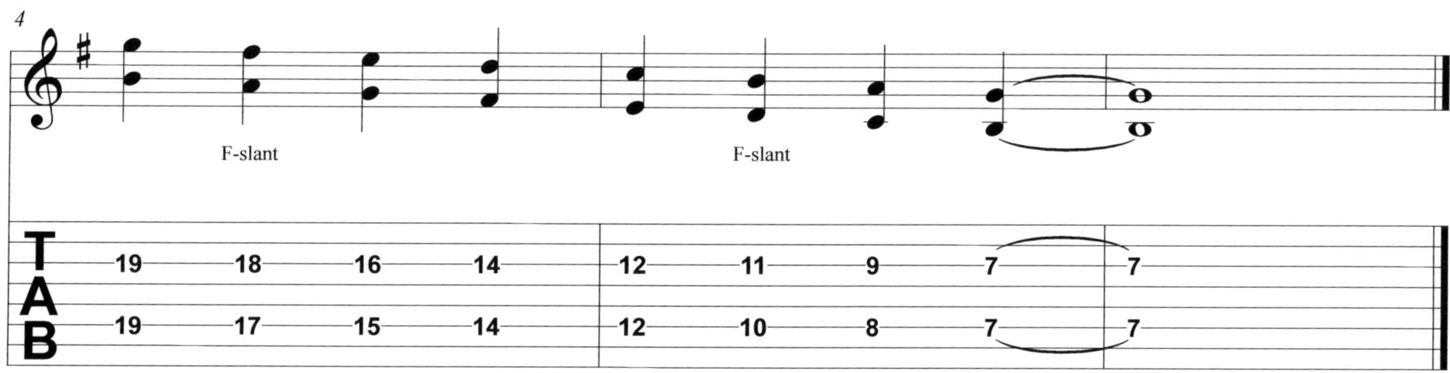

Here's another G scale with bar slants.

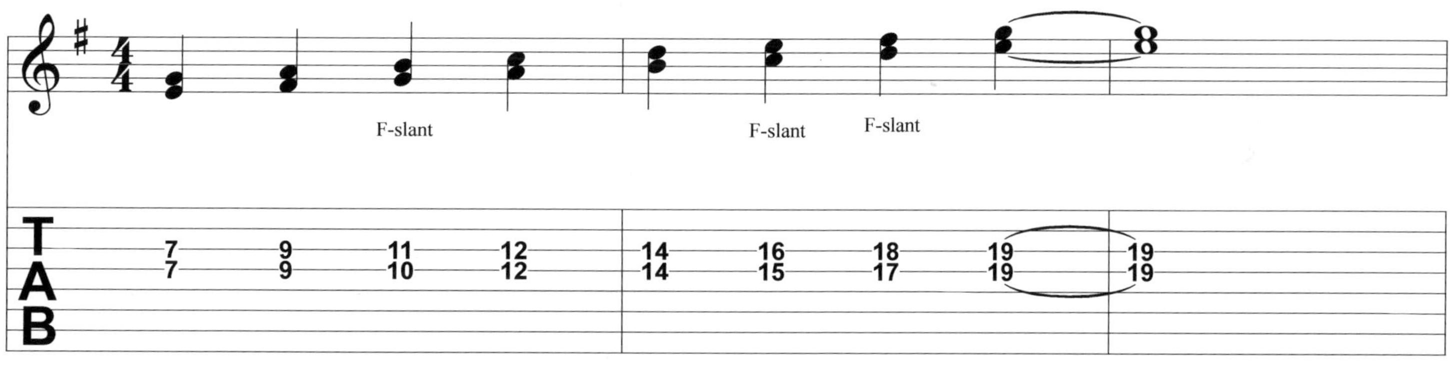

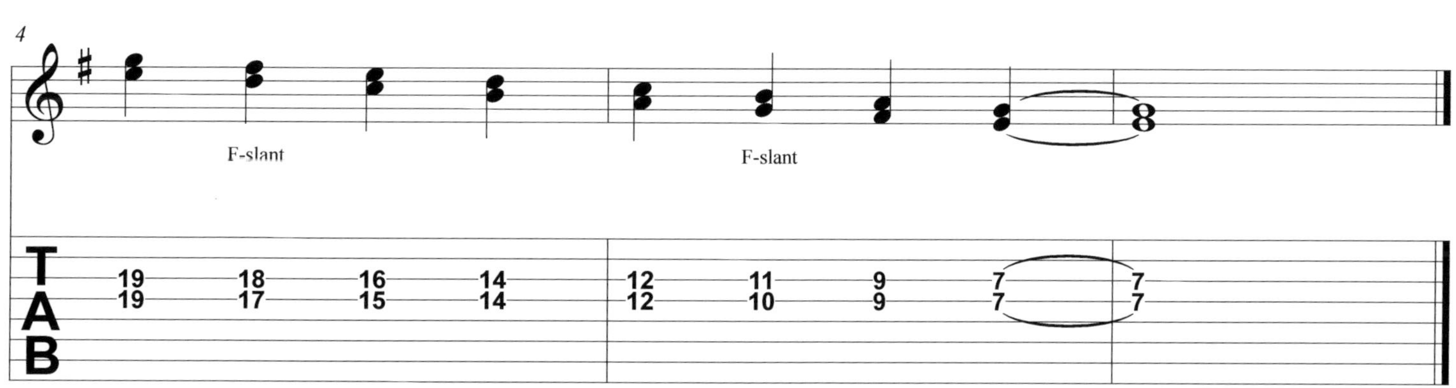

The Backward-Bar Slant (B-Slant) 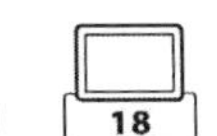

The thumb goes on the end or butt of the bar, closest to you. Use the thumb to slant the bar, pulling the end to a higher fret.

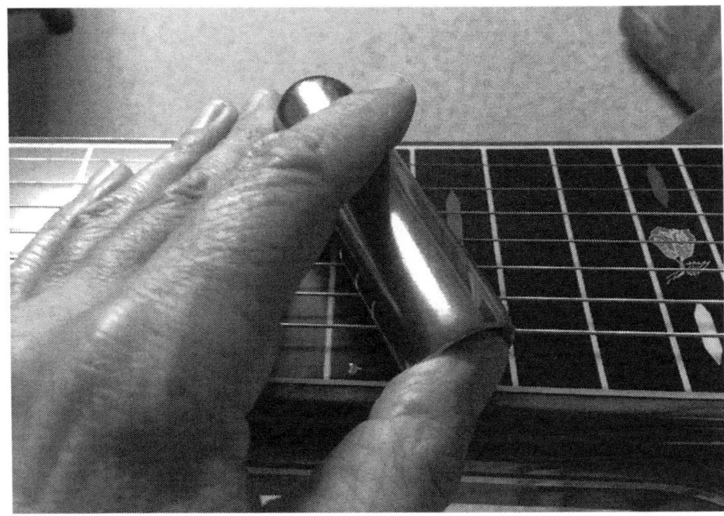

This first exercise is in the key of G on the 7th fret. In measure one, pick the 3rd and 6th strings. With first half note, the bar raises the 6th string to the 8th fret while holding the pitch on the 3rd string at the 7th fret. The second half note resolves the chord to the 7th fret. Practice going back and forth between the two chords. Work on a smooth slant and getting the chords to sound in tune. Measures 2 and 3 use this same backward slant and forward slant. Practice playing this lick in different keys at various frets. You will notice that as you move up the neck, the angle of the slants becomes less acute, while going lower on the neck requires a sharper angle.

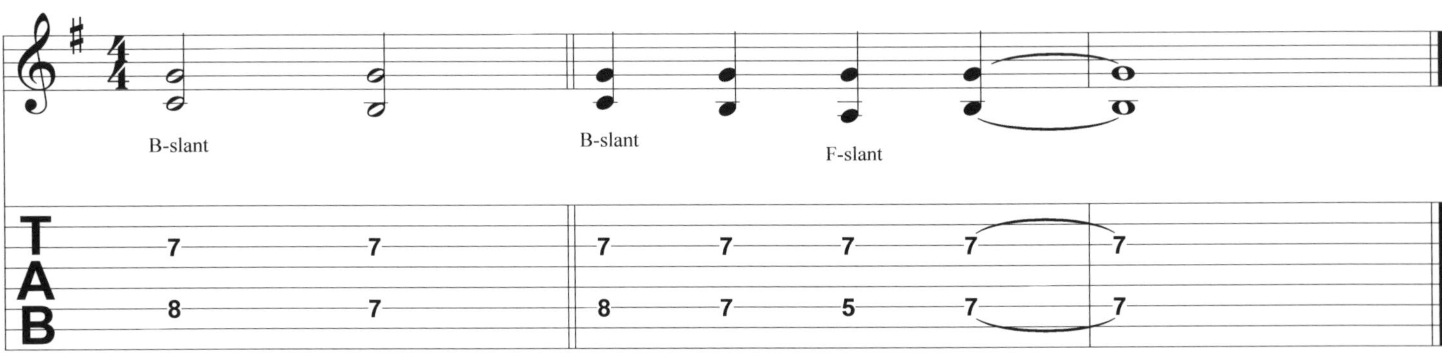

This next exercise is in the key of C. To get started, practice just the first measure, going back and forth between the two chords. The second chord is actually an F chord. So you are going back and forth between C and F, or the 1 and the 4 chord in the Nashville Number System. On a pedal steel guitar, this is a common lick using the “A” (first) and “B” (second) pedals. Once you become comfortable with this change, continue up the partial C scale and back down. Then, continue up the scale using your ear to decide where the bar goes and slant versus no slant. Finally, practice in different keys.

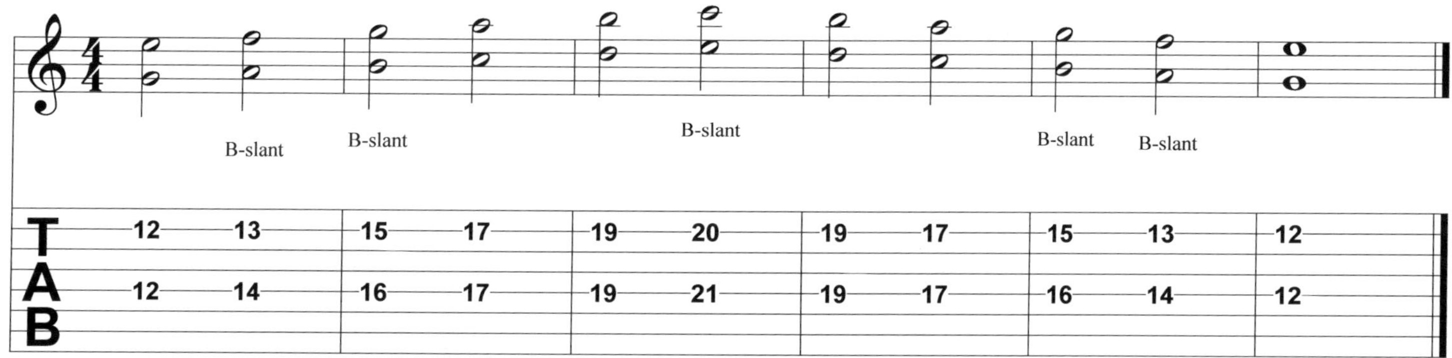

Don Helms-Style Intros

Everyone has heard this intro, very straight ahead. It's called a **5 5 5 1** intro, three measures of G, the 5 chord, resolving to C, the 1 chord. Use the count below if you are playing in a band situation. I like to give at least 4 "beats" to establish the tempo. The 3rd and 4th quarter notes in the last measure of G are played with forward slants in the left hand and middle and thumb in the right.

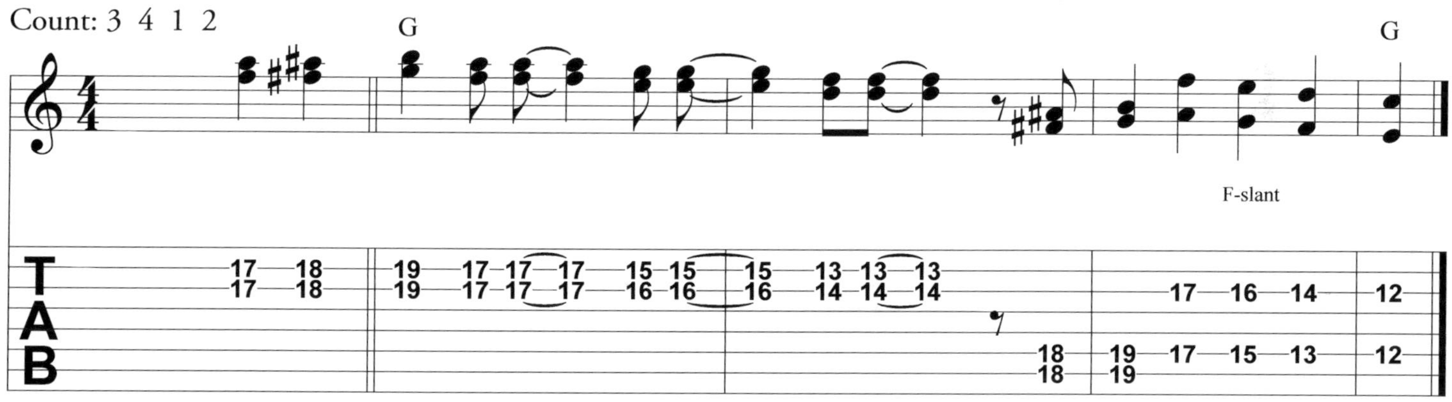

Here's another 5 5 5 1 intro that is similar. The right-hand fingerings are the same but with no bar slants. For the slide up, hit the chord on the 11th fret and slide it up to the 12th.

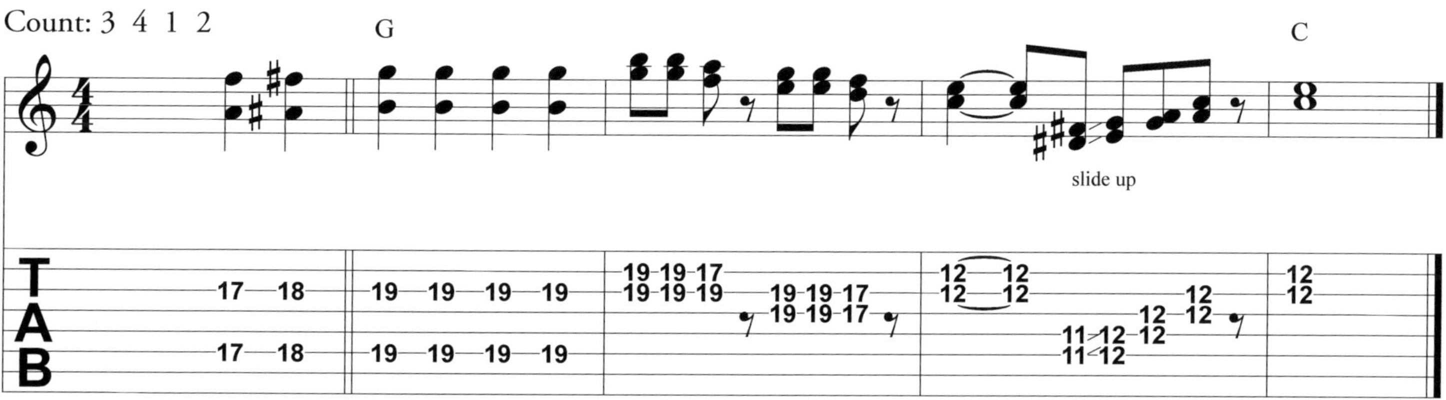

Another Don Helms intro; everyone will recognize this one—**2 5 1 5** intro in the key of B♭. The tab looks simple, but it's harder to play in tune when you are high up the neck. So practice playing in tune. Try it down an octave and in different keys.

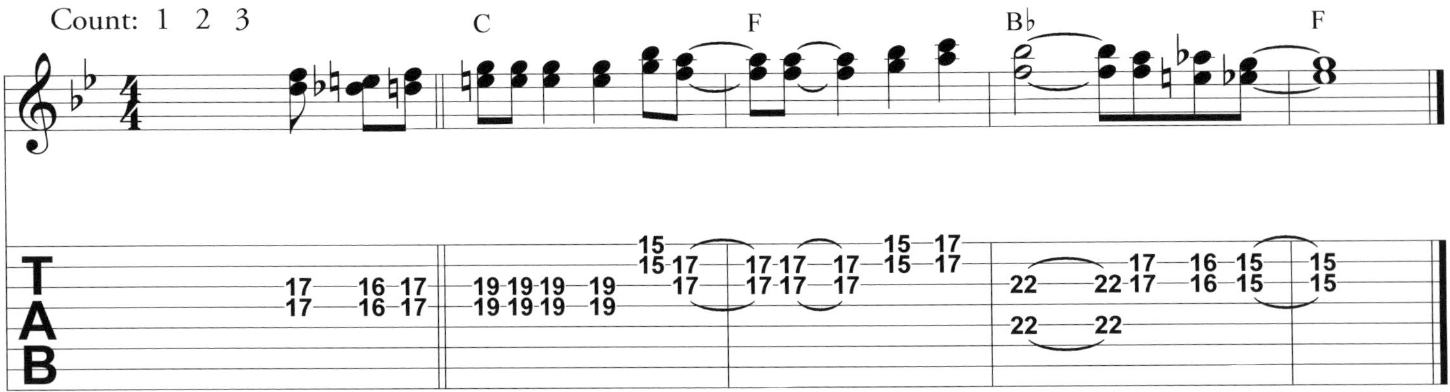

This intro is a **5 5 1 1** in the key of C with three pickup quarter notes. On the two chords that say "slide up" to the 12th fret, make it a quick slide from the 11th to 12th fret.

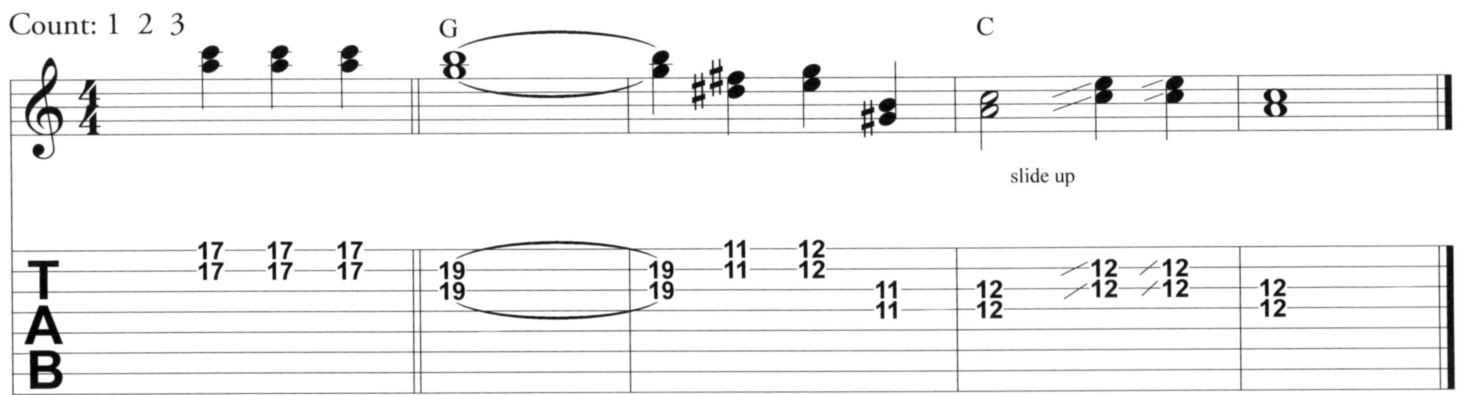

Minors Using Bar Slants

Place the bar at the 7th fret, where all of the notes on strings 2-5 form a G^6 chord. The notes consist of B, G, E and D. If you play only the 2nd, 3rd and 4th strings, that chord is an Em. The two chords are very close; the only difference is that Em has no D. In the key of G, Em is called the relative minor or 6m. The 6m is the most commonly used minor in chord progressions.

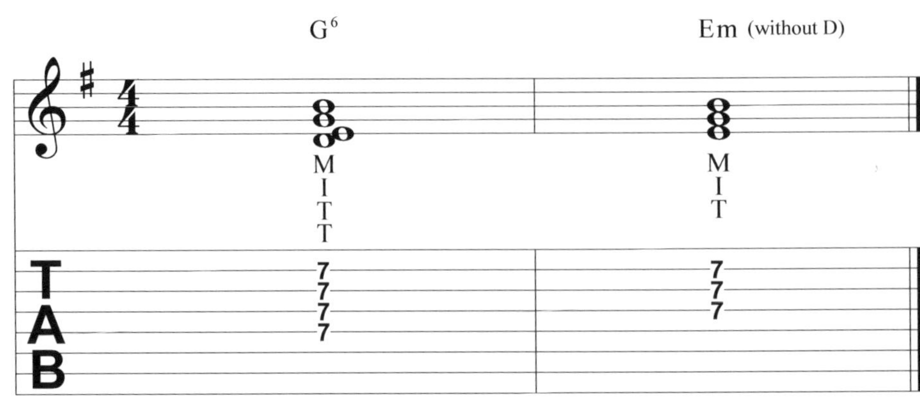

The Em chord in the first measure below takes the E away from the bottom of the chord and adds it to the top. Try playing this chord with a forward bar slant. It's not easy to make it sound in tune and takes a lot of practice. Practice going from Em on the 7th fret to the one below and back slowly. Work on making the bar slant sound in tune. On slow songs, it's easier to do the three-string bar slant because once you hit the chord and it doesn't sound in tune, you can adjust the slant and make it sound better. On faster songs and licks, use two-string versions of the Em. Practice these as well. Finally, practice everything in different keys with different chords.

12-fret bar slant

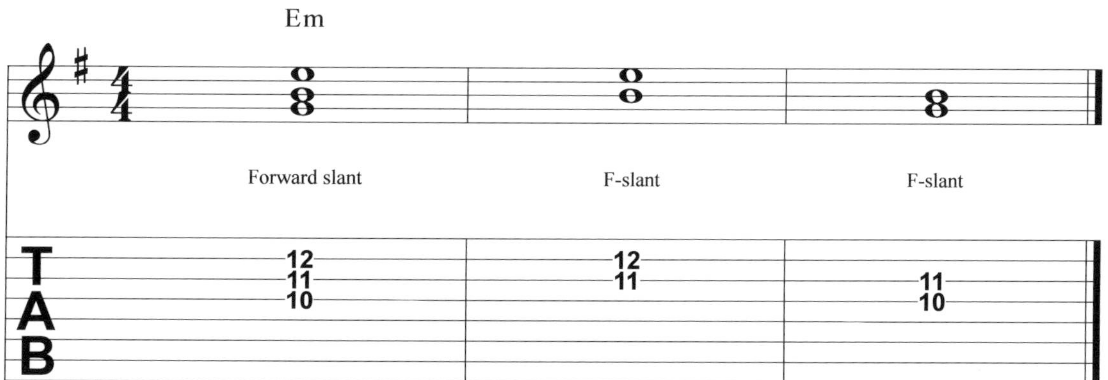

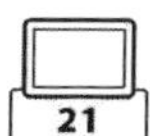

Let's examine the **G^7 string pull** at the 7th fret. In this position, it's very common to pull the 4th string with the ring finger, raising the 6th in the chord to the 7th or dominant seventh. It takes some practice, your finger may hurt a little at first, until you get a callus. If it really bothers you, consider getting a lighter gauge string for the 4th. The tablature says it's the 8th fret, but it's really the 7th with the pull.

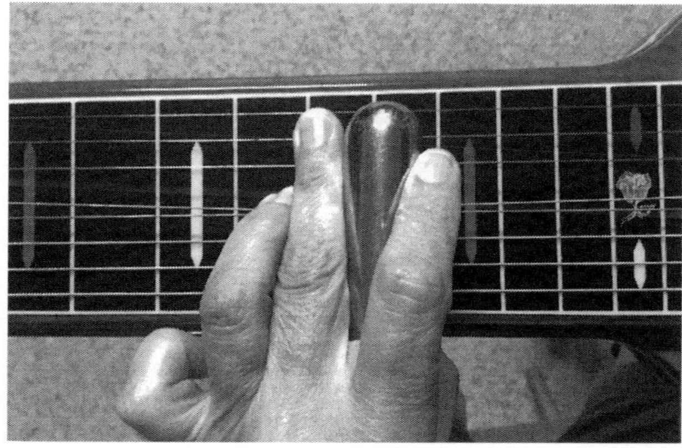

The Fender Champion was a very popular lap steel made from 1949 to 1955, when it was replaced by the Champ which was made through 1980.

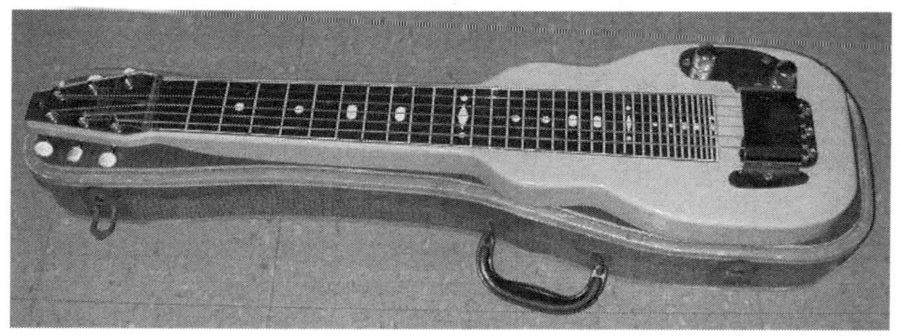

The A^6 to A^7 lick

As we've already established, placing the bar across all strings at the 9th fret makes the A^6 chord. This lick uses the same right-hand string grips, 3rd, 4th, and 5th throughout. The first chord is an A^6, of course. The second chord move this up to the 12th fret. Hit the chord and use your left-hand ring finger to pull the 3rd string up to that C♯. This will make the chord an A7. Play the 2nd string at fret 12 all on its own, then go back to the 9th fret. Don't let the sharp, flat and natural signs scare you. It's just walking the G^6 up with a syncopated rhythm. Practice this lick in different keys. Make up your own licks using this idea with different rhythms and chords.

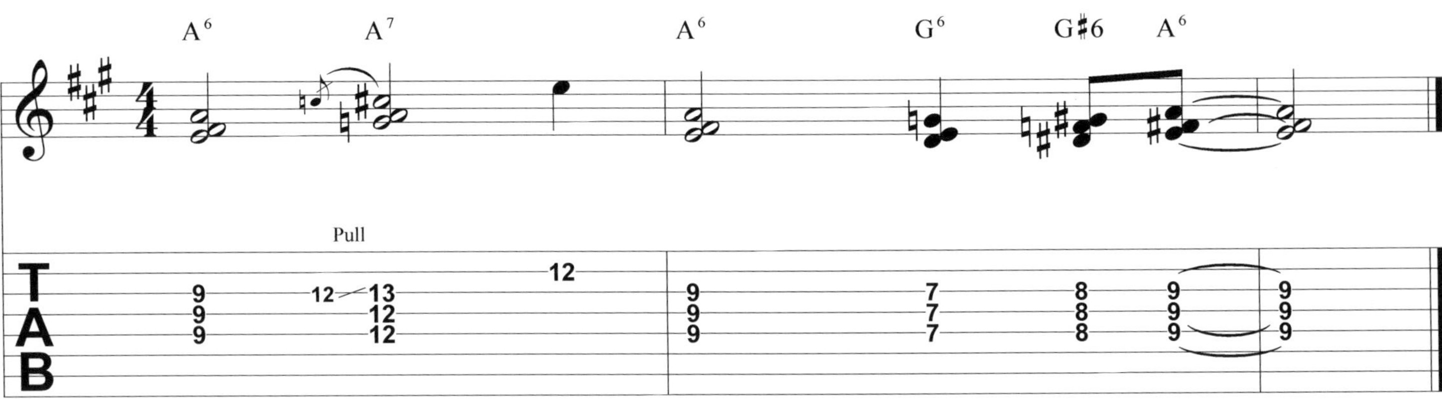

Take this lick and chord grip a step further and add the 16th fret. The music below will get you started. Use the chords on the 7th, 9th, 12th, and 16th frets to create your own licks using the string pull on the 3rd string. You can pull it up and down the fretboard; get creative.

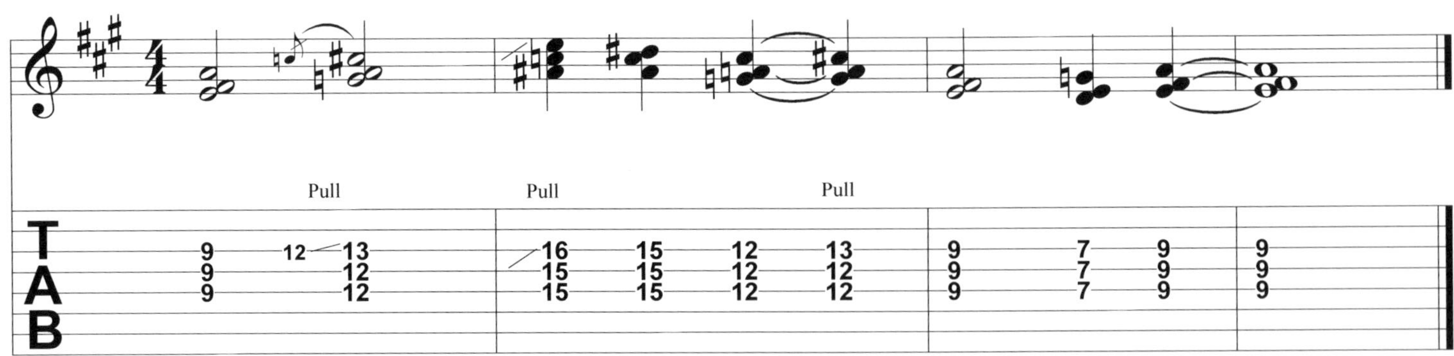

Effects Pedals

22

"Stomp boxes," pedals and rack-mounted effects can be fun but use them sparingly. Play around with some by taking your lap steel to a music store, or have a guitar-picking friend bring over his units for you to try. Distortion units or "fuzz tones" and blues drivers can be used while playing blues licks and bottleneck-type licks. Distortion pedals give a dirty, distorted sound while the blues driver is just slightly distorted. It simulates what an amp would sound like if cranked up so loud it causes distortion. The delay units are great for slow songs and can do a lot to hide bad intonation of faulty bar slants. Don't overdo it; too much sounds terrible. For slow songs I like to turn down the reverb a little and add a slight amount of delay. The best way to use a delay unit is to put it in between the guitar and volume pedal. So the signal goes guitar to delay to volume pedal to reverb to amp. Digital reverb can sound better than the amp's built in reverb, and you don't have to worry about the springs crashing during a performance. That can be embarrassing or funny, depending on the setting. Play around with other types of effects like chorus, phase shifter, wah-wah and more. There are a lot of new types of effects units; that's why I recommend that you go to a music store and have a salesman let you try what's new.

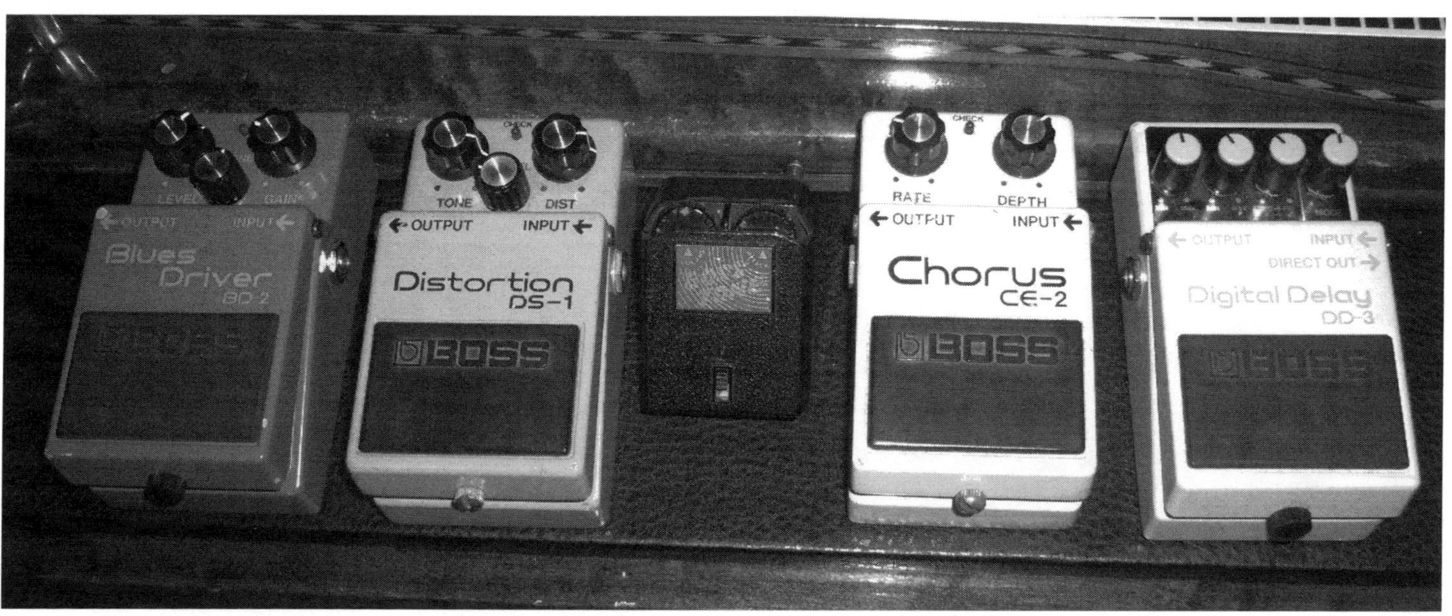

Blues Scale 

The blues scale contains some notes not found in the major scale. Technically speaking, there are several types of blues scales but we are going to cover the most common one. It's often used by rock guitar players and others.

C major scale: C, D, E, F, G, A, B
C blues scale: C, E♭, F, F♯, G, B♭

There are three notes in the blues scale that are not found in the major scale:

E♭ – the flat third
F♯ – the sharp fourth
B♭ – the flat seventh

The flat third and flat seventh are considered the main "blue notes." The blues scale in the key of C appears below and in G on the second staff. Notice that the first note of the C scale (the tonic) can be played on the 3rd string open or on the third fret of the 4th string.

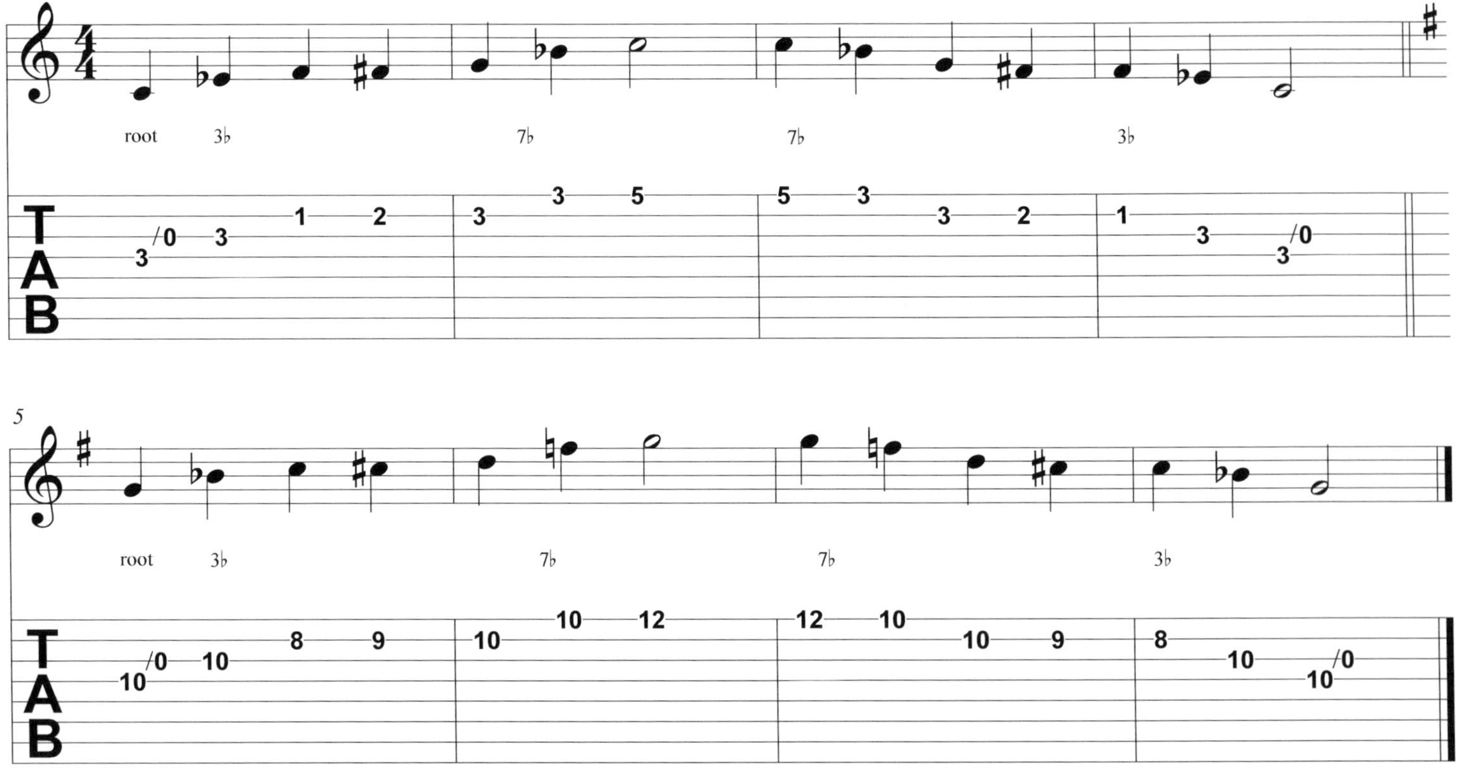

Slide or bottleneck licks can use notes from the blues scale and blue notes. This first lick uses triplet eighth notes. Practice tapping your foot for quarter notes and saying or playing 1-2-3, 2-2-3, etc. with three eighth notes to the quarter. Slide up where notated and try using heavy vibrato to produce a cool sound.

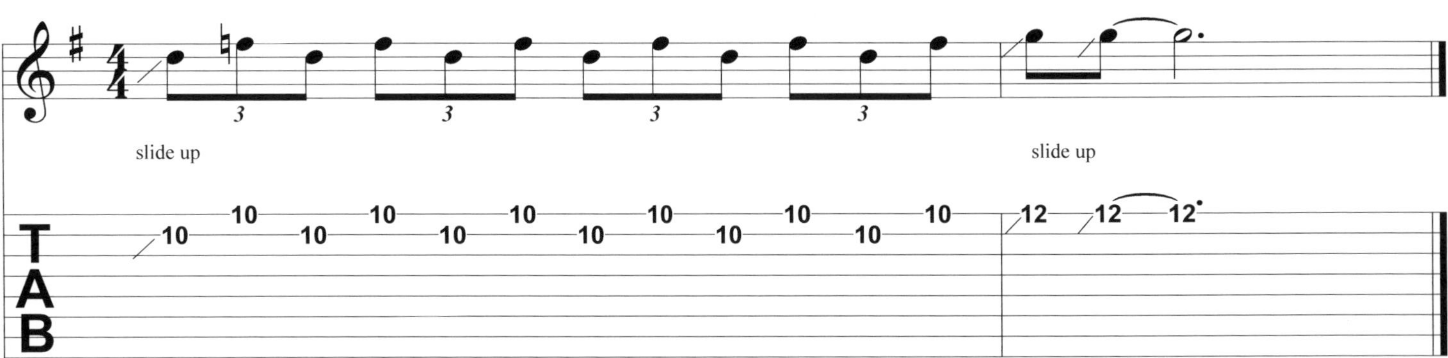

Here's a similar lick based on the triplets.

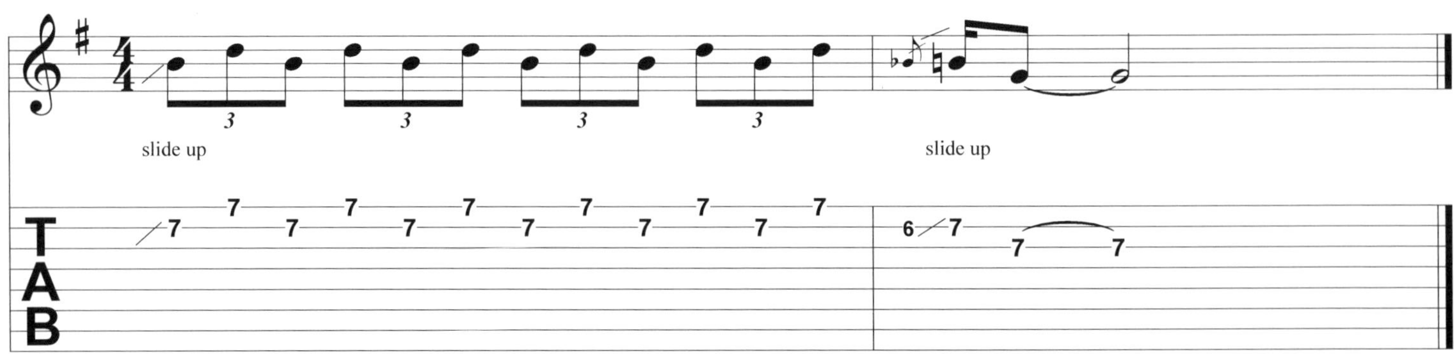

Here's a variation of the previous lick. You can play it as written, but what I like to do is slide the bar down slowly for the first measure, playing the half steps in between the written notes. Steel guitar is one of the few instruments that let you do this. Keep the vibrato heavy. That grace note in the second measure could be written as a simple slide. You can vary the amount of time that you slide up from the B-flat to the B-natural.

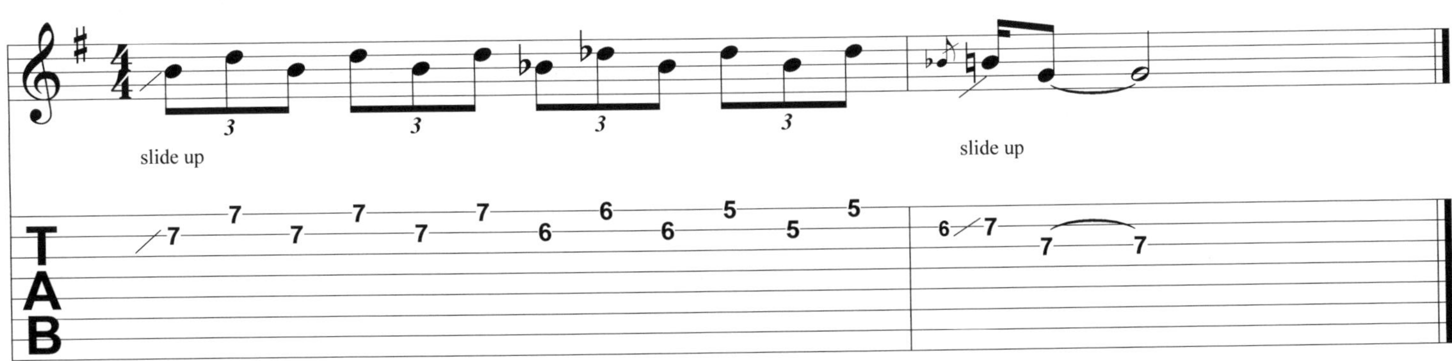

With this next one, slide up to the tonic note, then apply two fast slides down, slide back up to the flat third, then go back to the tonic. Use heavy vibrato.

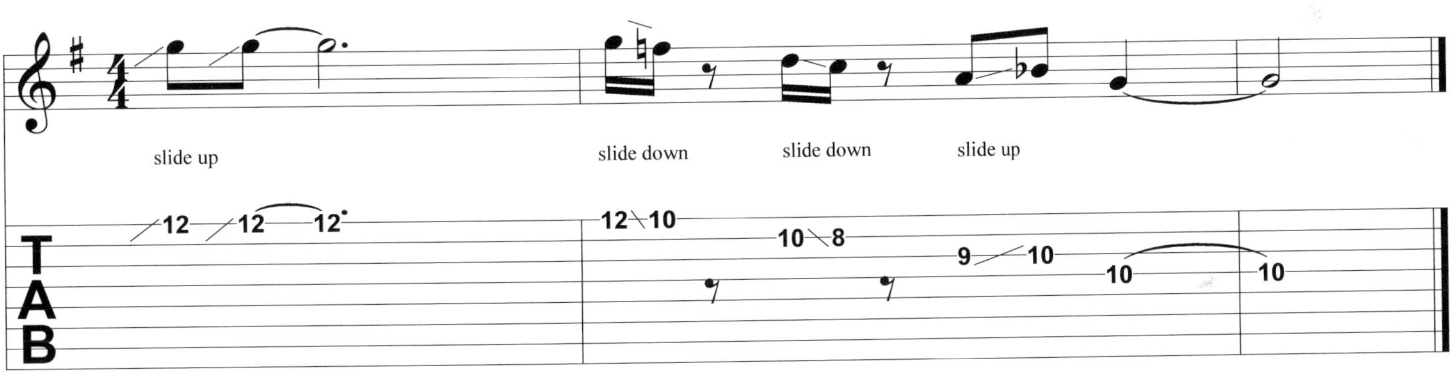

Experiment with these blues licks. Try different timing, different amounts of vibrato, different keys, etc. Mix them up and combine notes from the different licks. Come up with your own variations. Don't be afraid of hitting a bad note when you are practicing. That's how you learn.

Ave Maria

Yes, you can play classical music on a non-pedal steel guitar! This is a great tune that can double as a Christmas song. The first wo measures are a guitar intro that I included in case you play this with a guitar player.

In standard notation, sometimes you see a dot beside a note. The dot increases the duration of the note by one half of its original value. For instance, one half the value of a half note is a quarter note. Therefore, a dotted half note acquires the time value of a half note plus a quarter note. Similarly, the single dotted quarter note (F) in measure 3 gets one and a half beats. A second dot after a note adds half the value of the first dot, so the double-dotted quarter note, A in m. 3, gets one and ¾ beats.

When you see a small "3" over 3 notes, it indicates a triplet. In measure 11, the sixteenth note triplets get the same time as 2 sixteenth notes. Think of counting 1-2-3 for each beat. The small "6" above the notes indicates a sextuplet, a note grouping of six, which is played within the duration of four of its note-type.

Note that on the video I have taken some liberties with the timing of the melody. That is, some notes are not played exactly as written in terms of note duration.

Franz Schubert

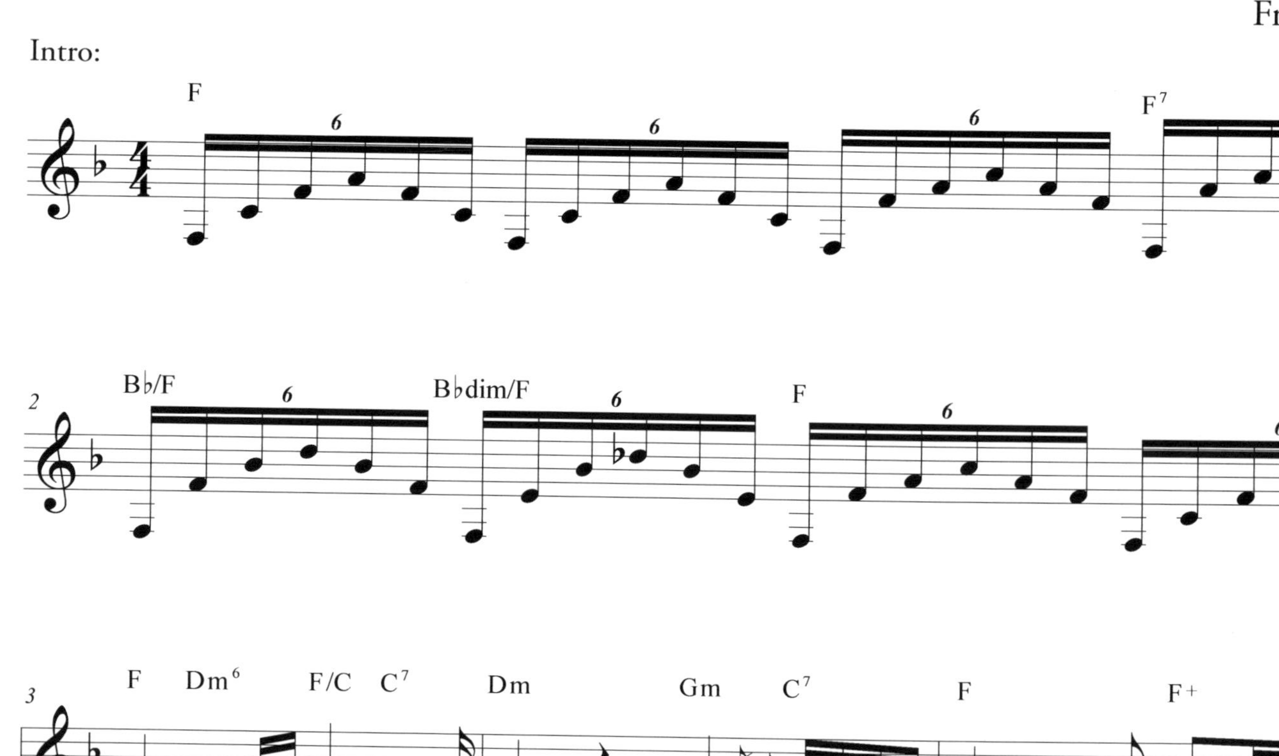

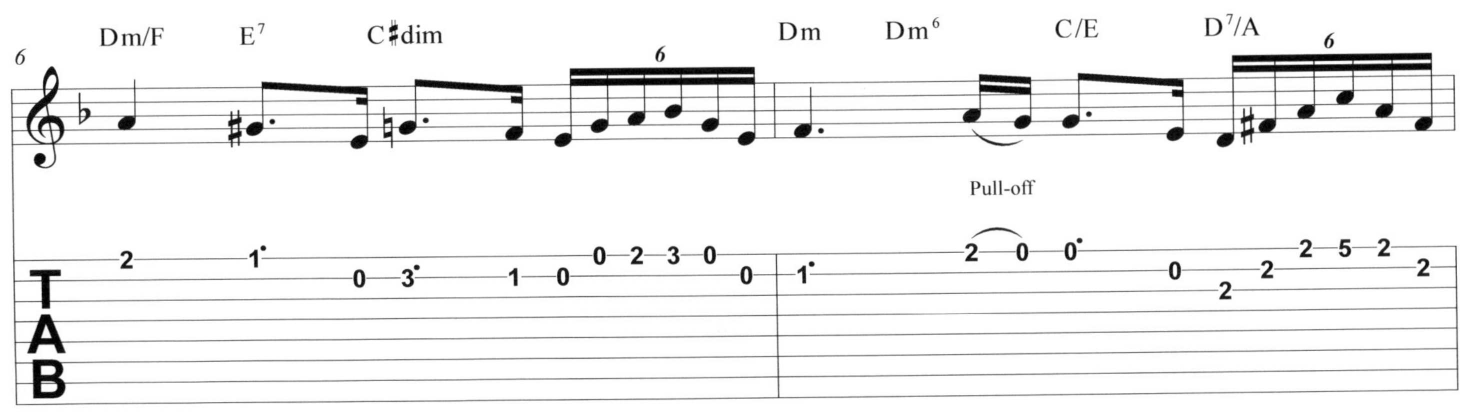

6
Dm/F
E7
C♯dim
Dm
Dm6
C/E
D7/A
Pull-off
TAB

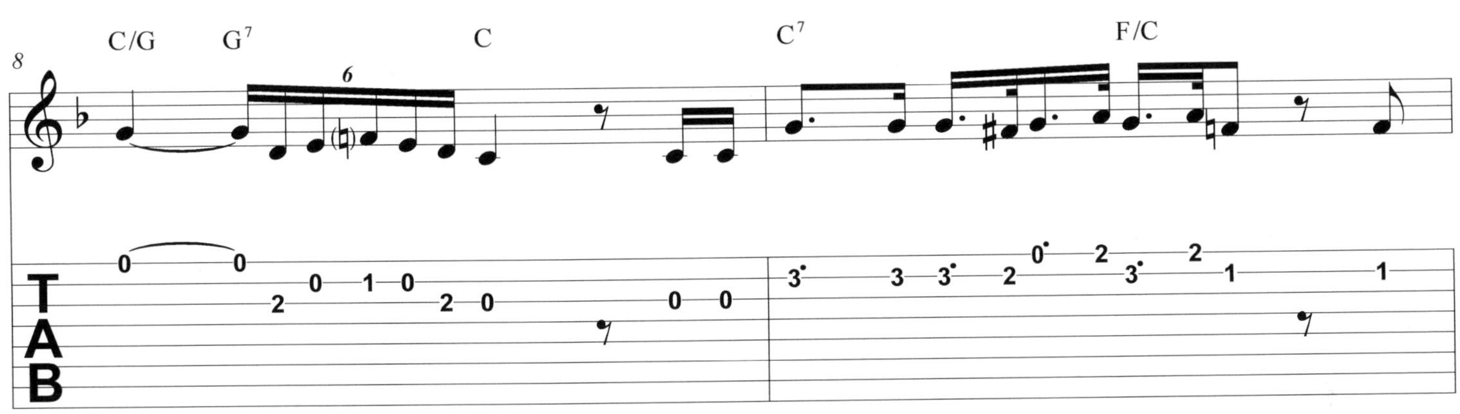

8
C/G
G7
C
C7
F/C
TAB

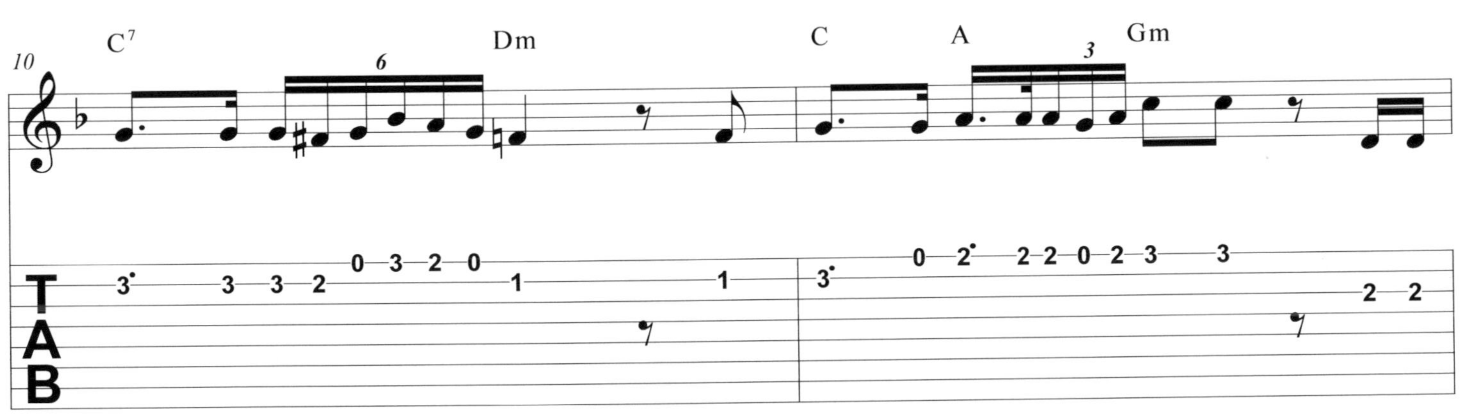

10
C7
Dm
C
A
Gm
TAB

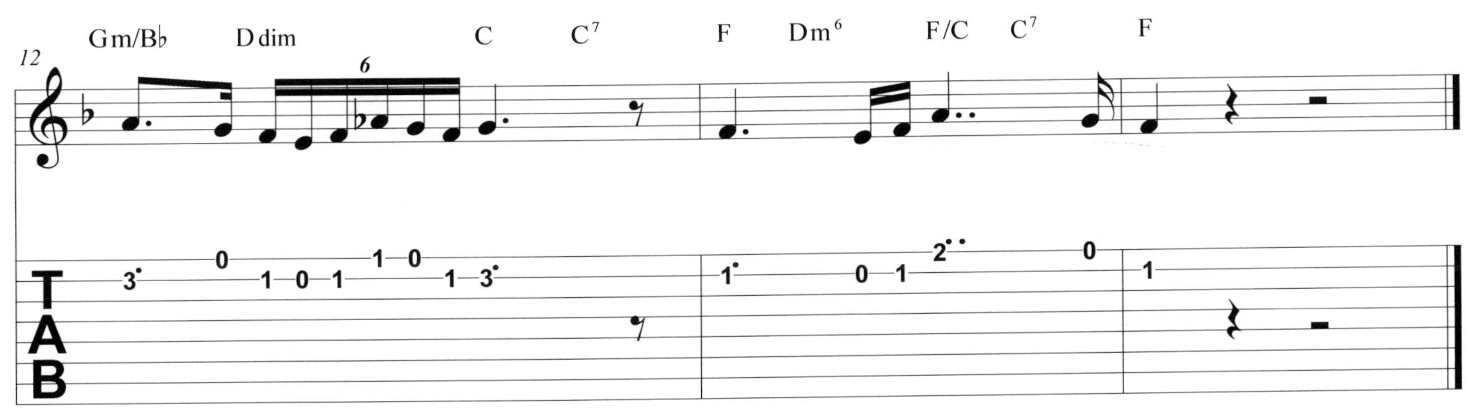

12
Gm/B♭
Ddim
C
C7
F
Dm6
F/C
C7
F
TAB

Advanced Bar Slants 

These bar slants can be tricky at first but are very cool. The second measure in "Advanced Bar Slant Lick 1" on page 42 is an F^6 chord, where the bar touches the 2nd string at the 10th fret, the 3rd string at the 9th fret and the 4th string at the 8th fret.

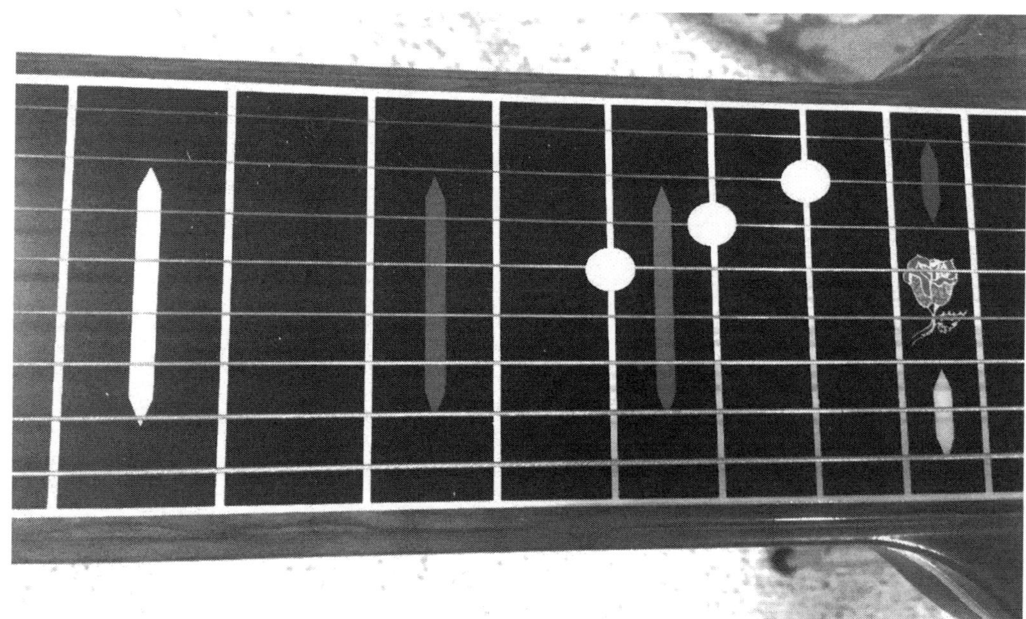

In the photo, I have moved my fingers back so you can see what the bar position looks like. The right-hand picks thumb on the 4th string, index on the 3rd and middle on the 2nd string. Of course, it's hard to make it sound in tune at first. Practice, practice. It will come in time.

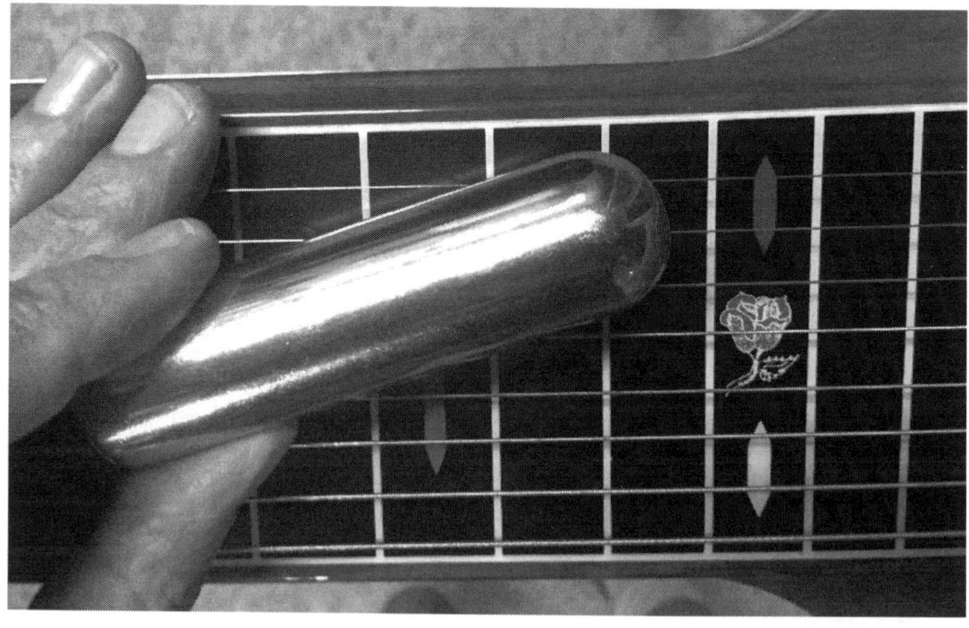

The third measure in Lick 1 features the F^+ or F augmented chord. From the previous position, rotate your hand and bar counterclockwise a little. The "nose" of the bar catches the 3rd string at the 9th fret and the 4th string at the 9th fret as well. The body of the bar catches the 5th string at the 8th fret. Again, practice making these two chords, sliding from F^6 to F^+.

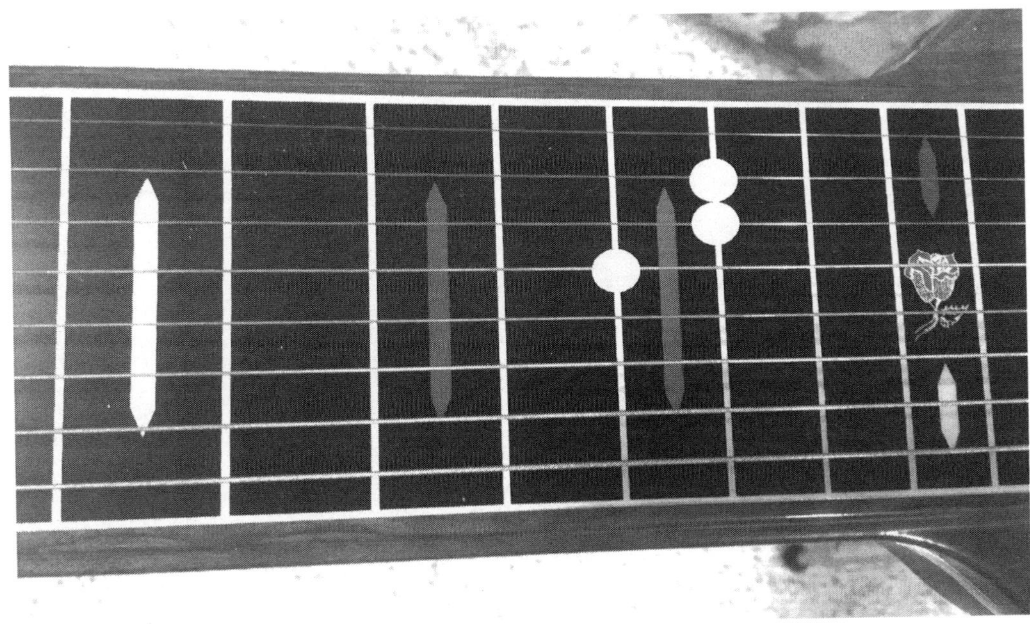

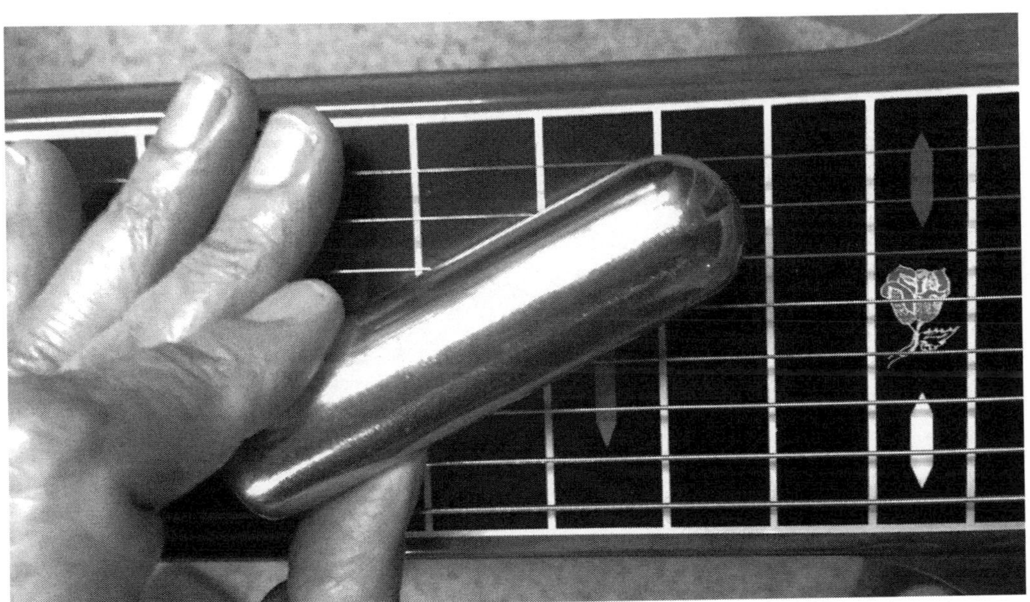

Advanced Bar Slant Lick 1

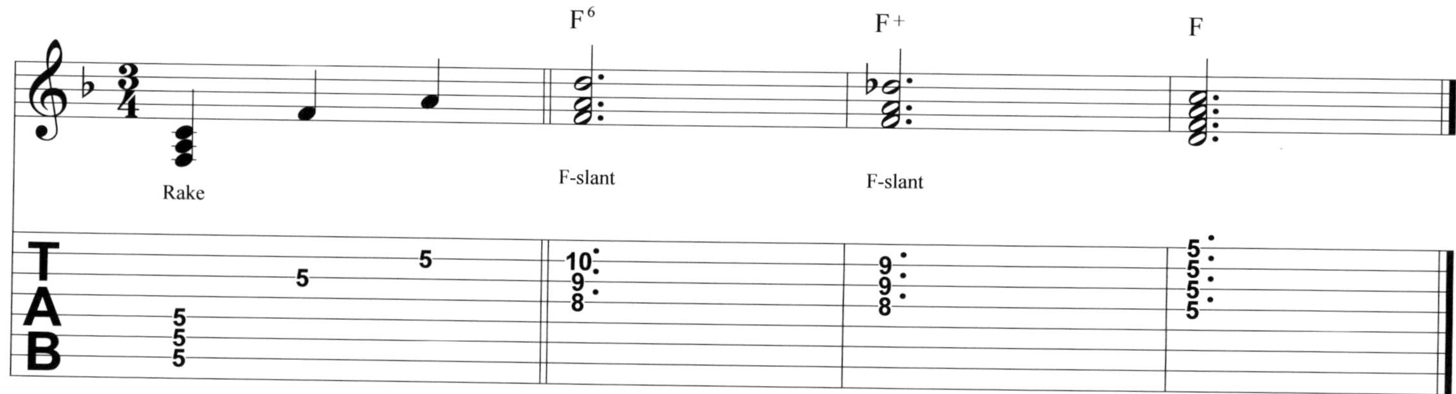

Nashville Number Chart

Key of F

3/4 | 1^6 1^6 1^+ 1

Advanced Bar Slant Lick 2

A lot of songs use a 1-5-1 chord progression, especially at the end of a verse or chorus. The example below does this using jazzy-sounding chords, the F^6 and C^+.

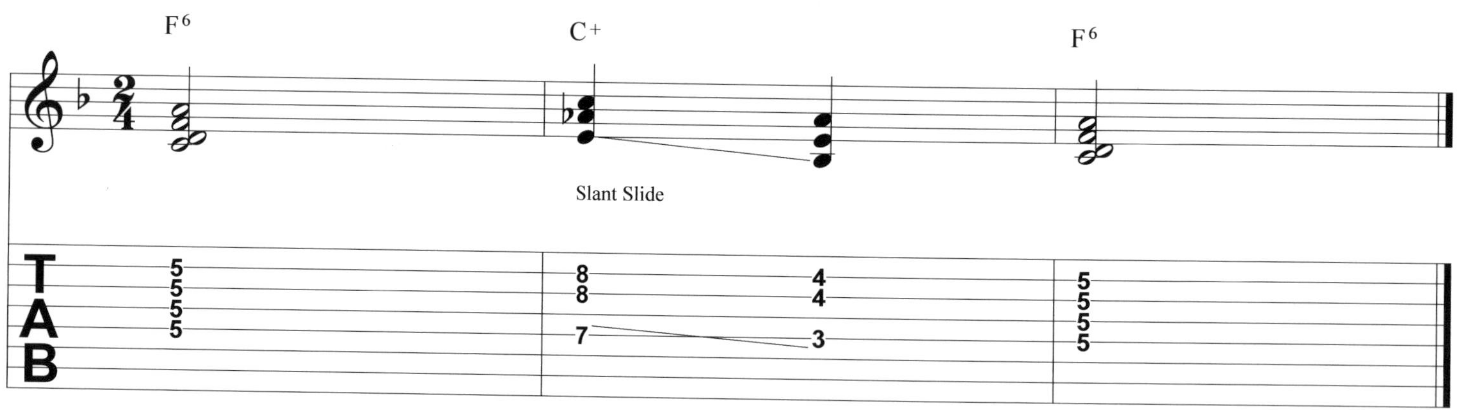

Key of F

2/4 | 1^6 5^+ 1^6

Advanced Bar Slant Lick 3

Here's a bar slant that works for the 5 chord resolving to the 1. The last chord in the C^7 measure is a cool and unique backward slant. This chord will never sound in perfect tune, but practice making it sound in tune as much as possible. During the actual performance of the song, it should go by fairly quickly.

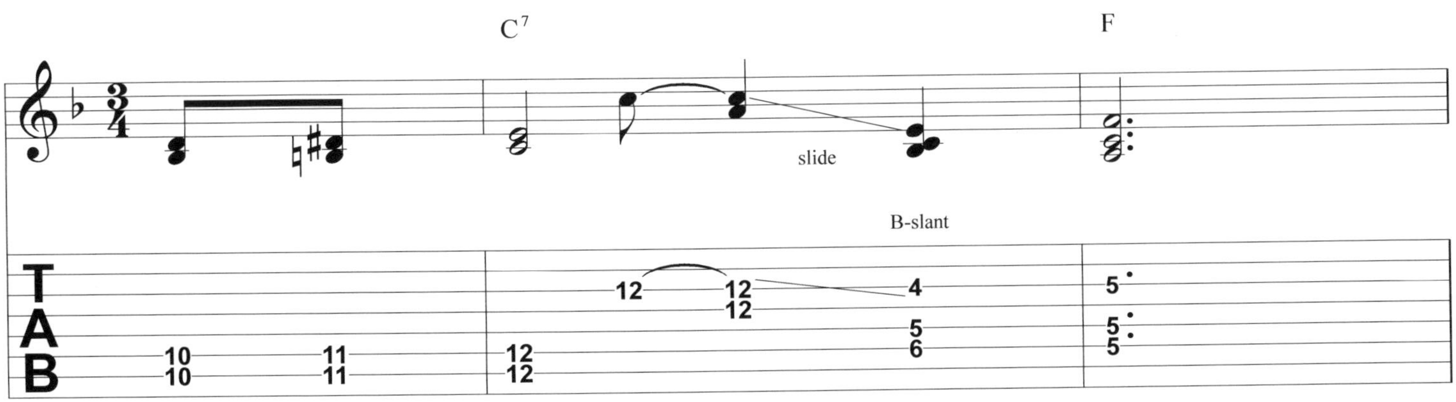

The Fender Stringmaster is a series of console steel guitars produced by Fender from 1953 to 1980. Models were available with two, three and four necks, each neck with eight strings. A single-neck version called the Fender Deluxe was also available in both six and eight-string versions. The guitars pictured here are not Stringmasters but use a very similar neck design and the same electronics configuration. The original 1953 models had a long scale length at 26". After 1954, the scale length was reduced and two shorter lengths were available. The shorter scale lengths are more desirable because bar slants are easier to execute on them.

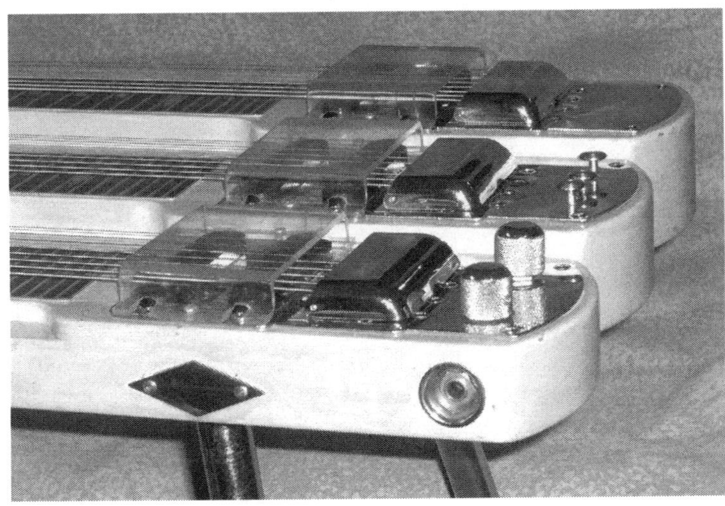

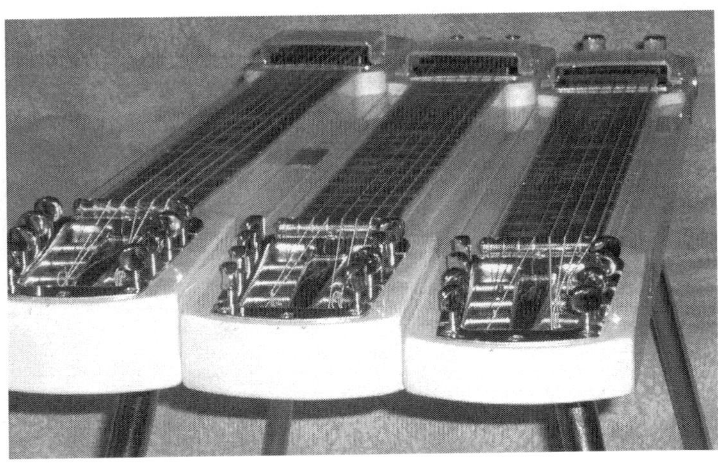

Jazzy-Sounding Lick 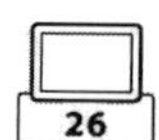

Here's a great-sounding lick using similar bar slants in the key of C. The top two notes, the E and C, are all on the 12th fret. So it's the bottom note of the chord that is sliding and slanting. In the last measure you can let the chord ring out.

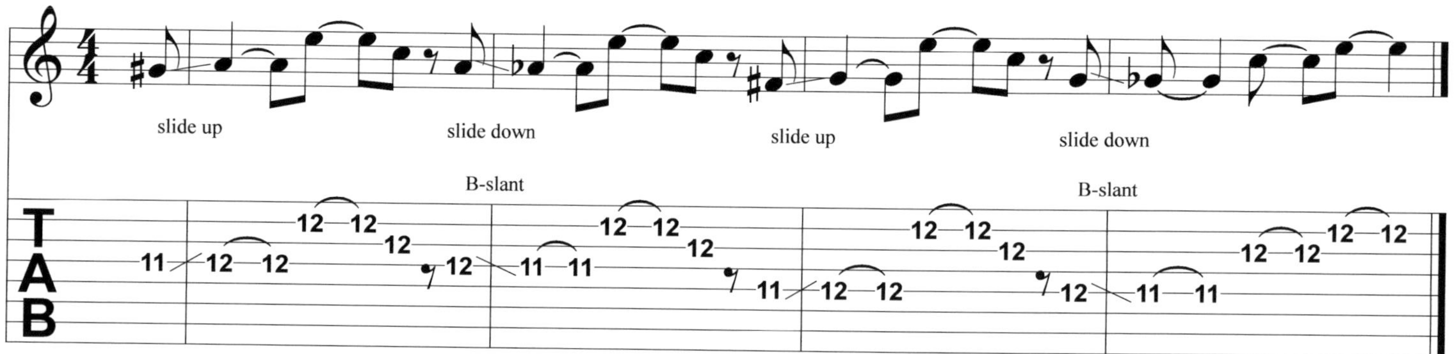

Hammer-On/Pull-Off Licks in D

These licks can open strings with the bar on the second or first fret. A hammer-on occurs when you pick the open 2nd string and hit the second fret with the bar. Pick only the first note, E; the bar hammer sounds the second note, F-sharp. Then immediately pull the bar off and the open string will ring. It's probably harder to explain this than to show it. Watch the video for more details. On these licks, the right-hand fingering is done with the middle finger and thumb.

Hammer-On/Pull-Off Lick 1

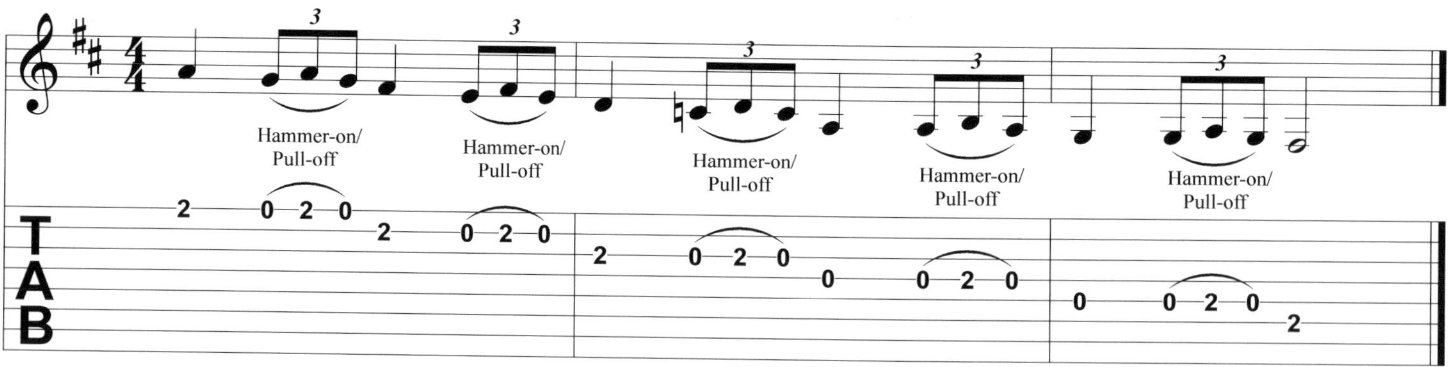

Hammer-On/Pull-Off Lick 2

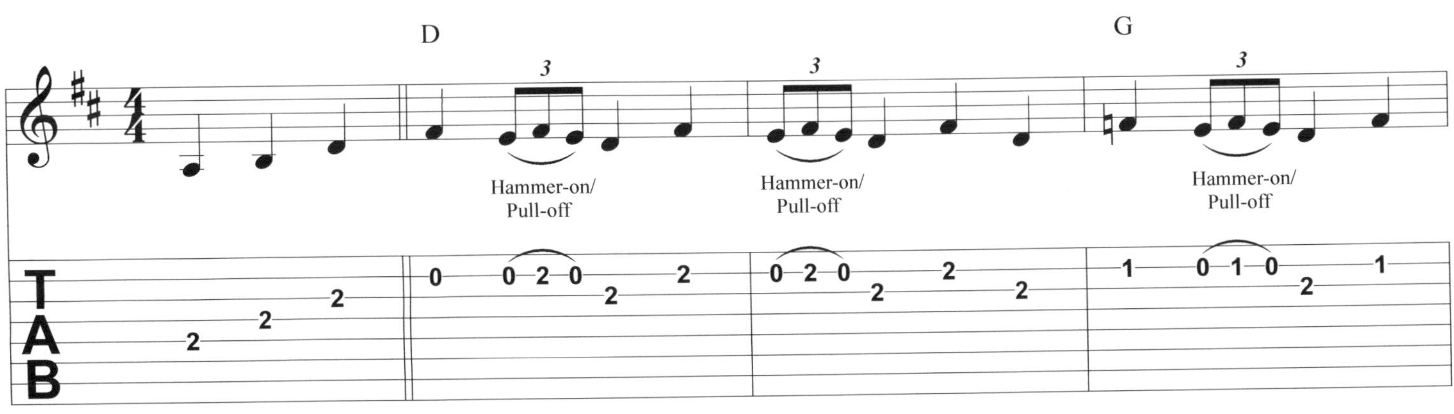

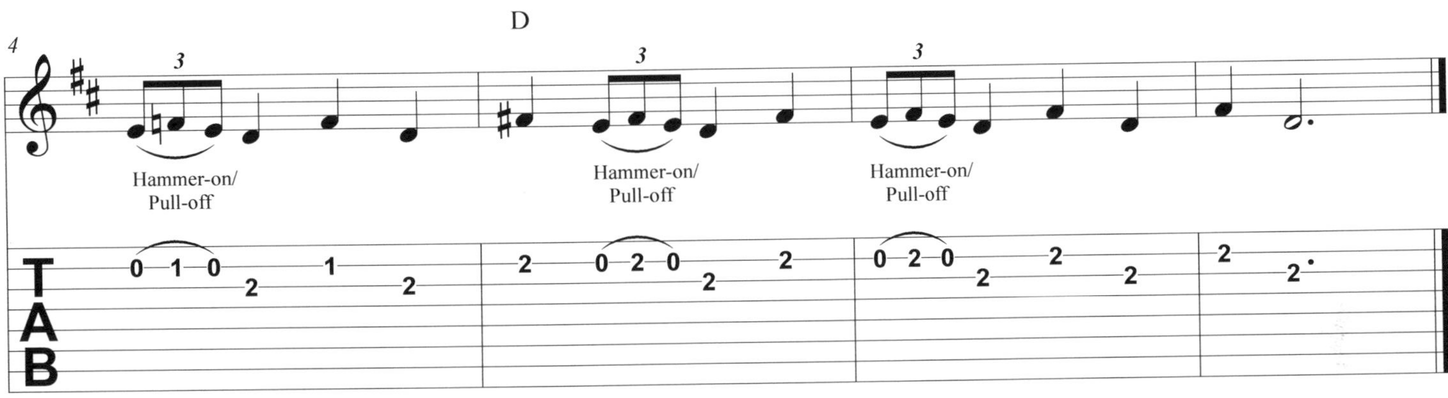

My Sierra SL-8 lap steel has legs so you could consider it a console, but it can be played either on one's lap or as a console. Some consider it the best-sounding and best-playing lap steel. It's hard to find used SL-8s and I'm not sure whether Sierra is still making these beautiful guitars.

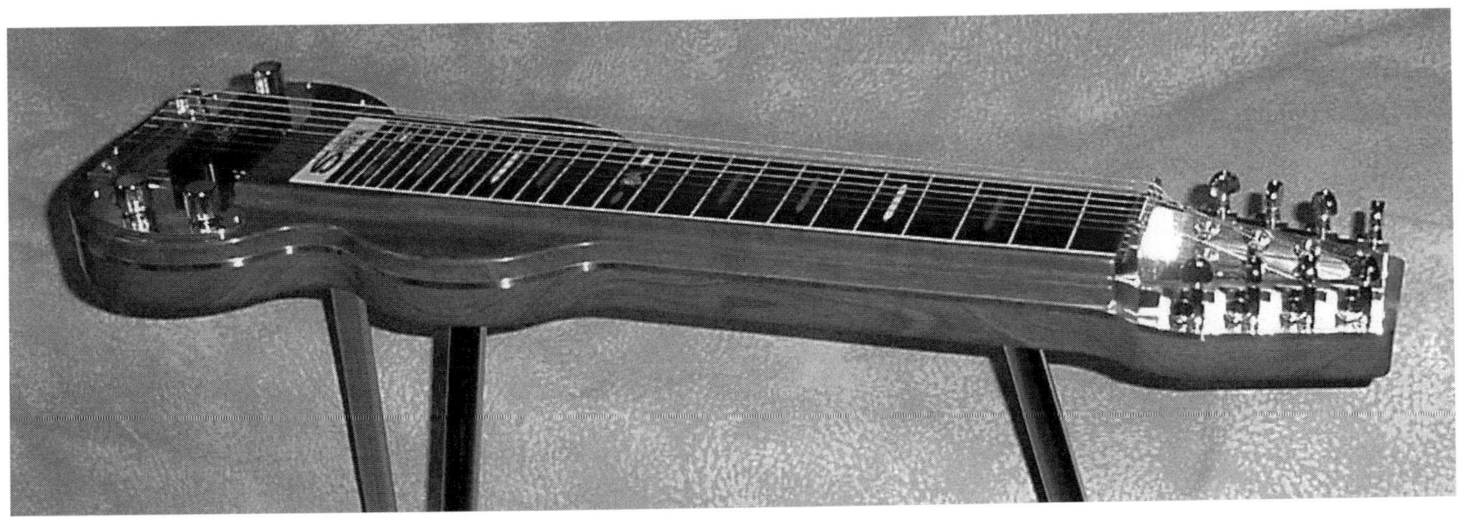

Hammer-On/Pull-Off Licks in C 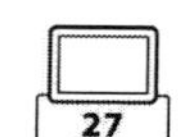

This lick bears a striking resemblance to "Guitar Rag" recorded by guitarist Sylvester Weaver in 1927, although others have mentioned its stylistic similarities to a popular Hawaiian song, "On the Beach at Waikiki" and others.

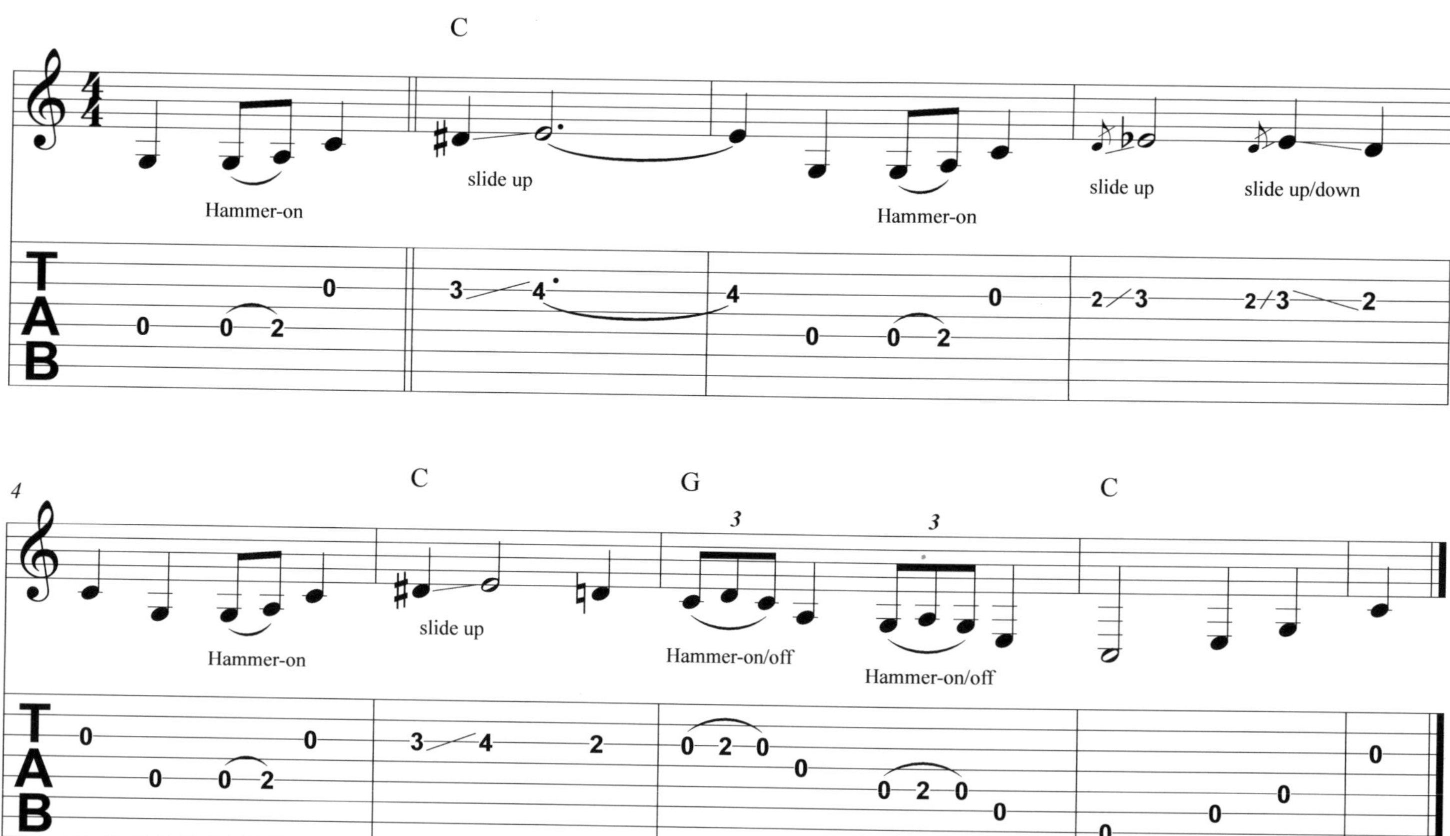

Chromatic Chord Ending Lick

This ending lick is very popular and can be played on virtually any instrument in any key. It's a 5 to 1 pattern. Hit the first G⁶ chord, slide down a half step and then slide up one fret at a time until you end up on C⁶. Use lots of vibrato on the last chord.

Note in the ending it says "free time." Most bands stop and let the steel play this by itself. "Free time" means there is no discernible beat. Instead, the rhythm is intuitive and free-flowing.

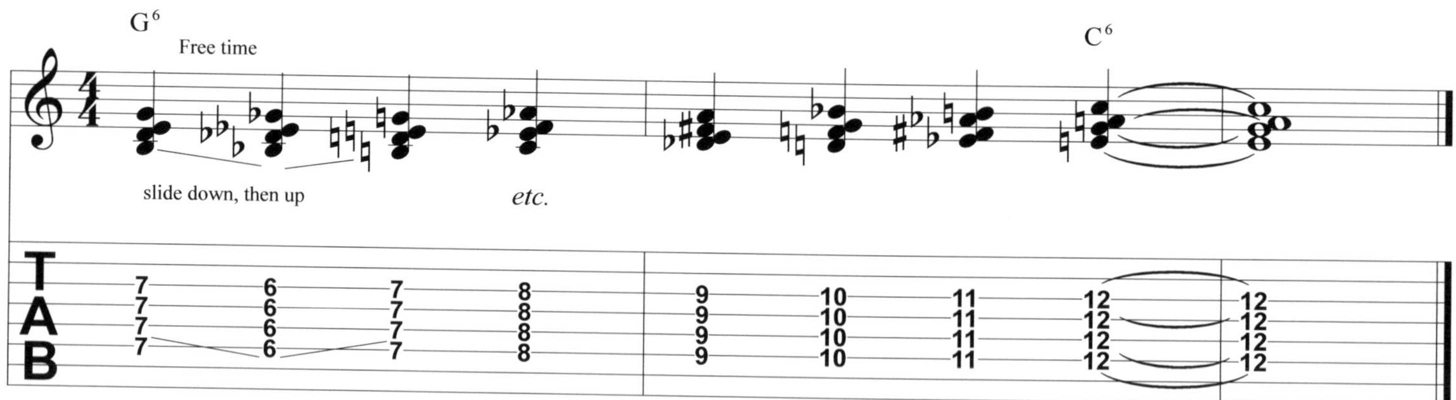

Fake Pedal Steel Intro #1

Some people call these intros or licks "fake pedal steel licks." That's because they simulate what the pedal steel does and sound as if you're using pedals. It's a 1, 5, 1 intro in the key of C. When you see a slide up or slide down, pick the note and slide to the next without picking the next note. That last grace note to half note can either be a forward bar slant or a string pull. Practice it both ways.

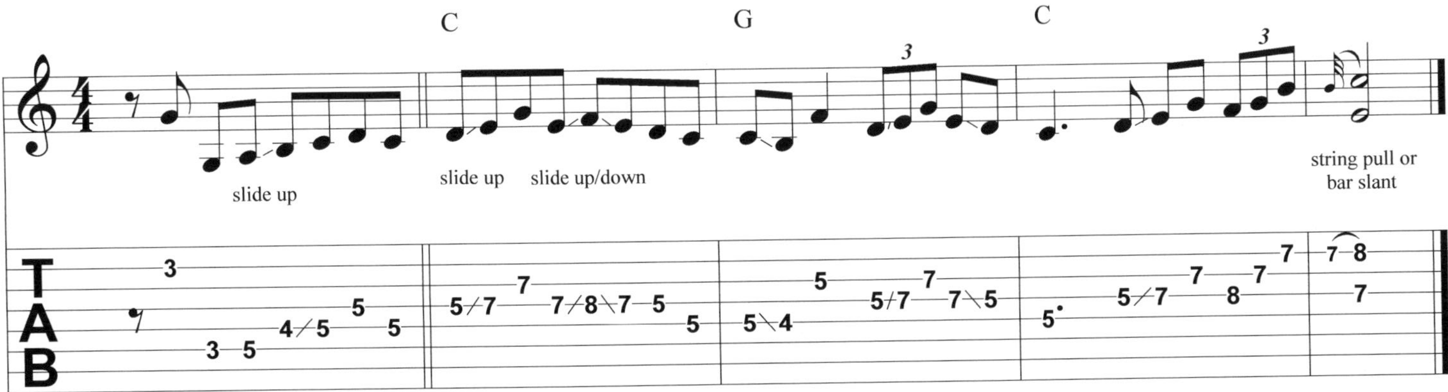

Fake Pedal Steel Intro #2

Here's another one. It's a 5511 intro in the key of G. It can also be used as a turn-around or lick. Pick the last three notes, the two eighth and the following half notes with middle, index and thumb. Let the three notes ring to get that cool-sounding G⁶ chord.

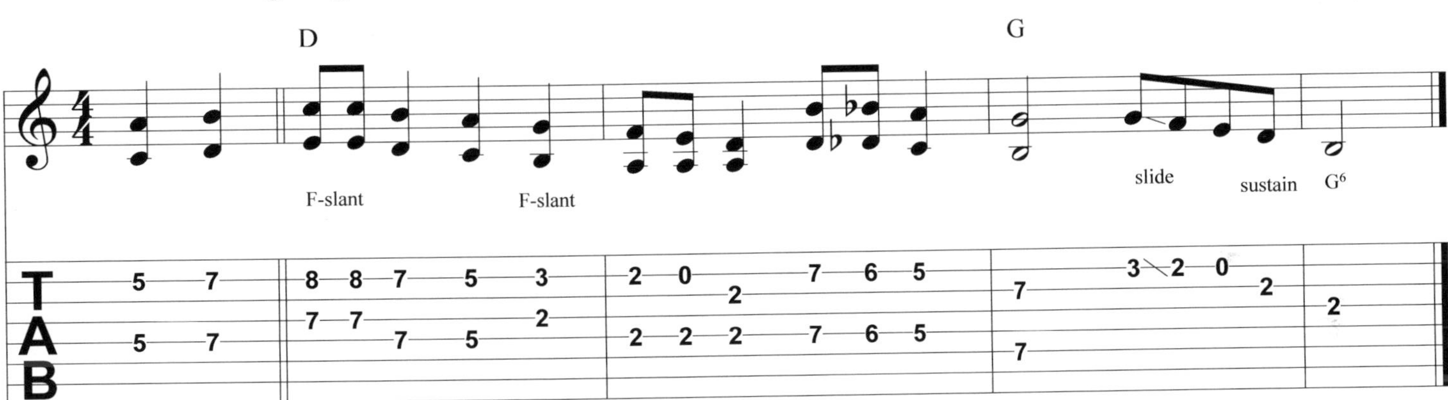

Jerry Byrd-Style Ending Lick

This is also a typical ending in a lot of different styles of music. Hit the first chord and slide everything up. Start slow. It will take lots of practice to get the intonation right with the bar slants.

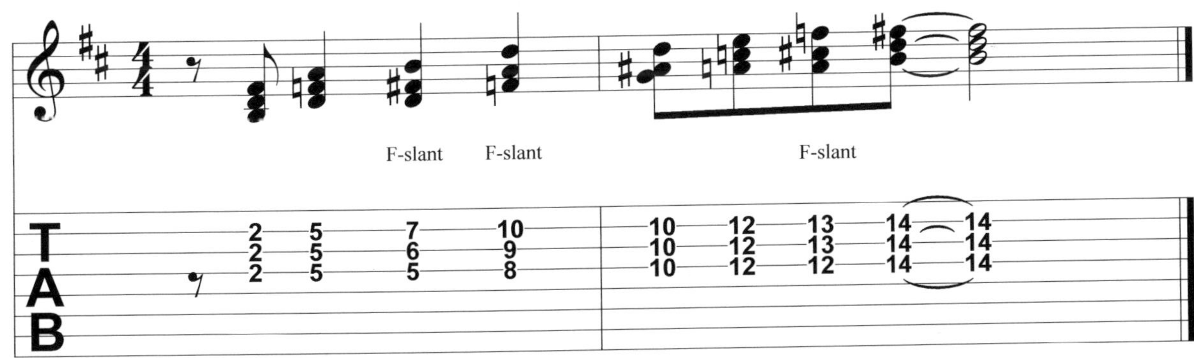

Ending Lick from D to G

All of the 0-2-0 frets figures are played the same way. Hit the string open, hammer-on to the second fret, then pull-off back to the open string. The right-hand fingerings are all the same as well.

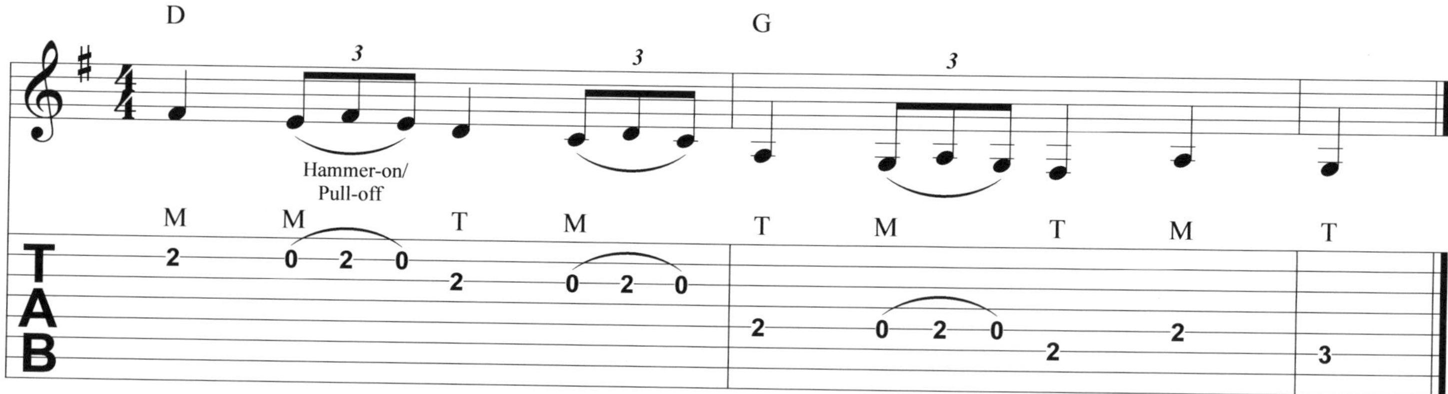

Ending Using Harmonics Only

Here's a cool-sounding lick that uses harmonics on a the 12th, 19th and 24th frets. Since these are all harmonics, the actual notes being played sound an octave higher than written. I use my left-hand pinky to get the notes, but you could use the ring finger. As discussed in the previous harmonics section, the finger lightly touches the string. If you touch the string too firmly, the harmonic will sound muted.

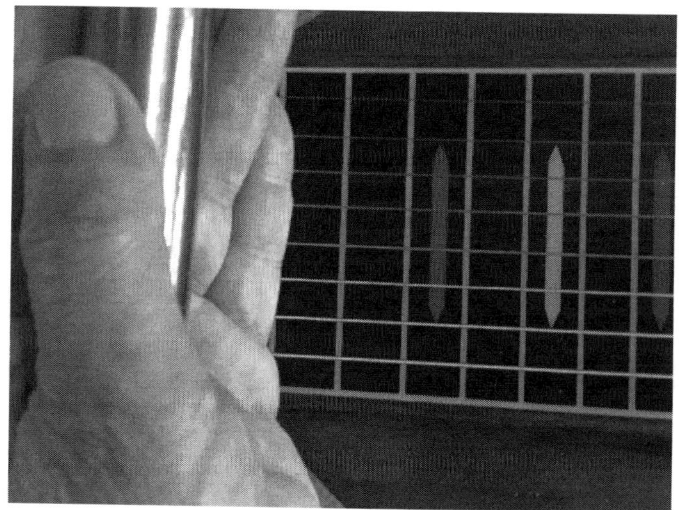

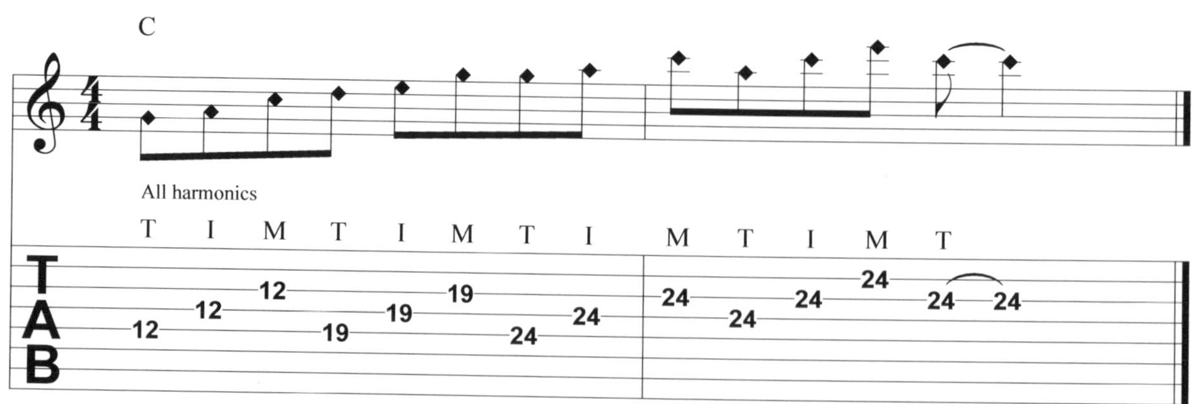

Intro Using Full Sixth Chords

29

Hit the E⁶ chord and slide down. Repeat on different strings. Then walk up from A^6 to B^6 chromatically. The tune starts at the fourth measure in E with no chords.

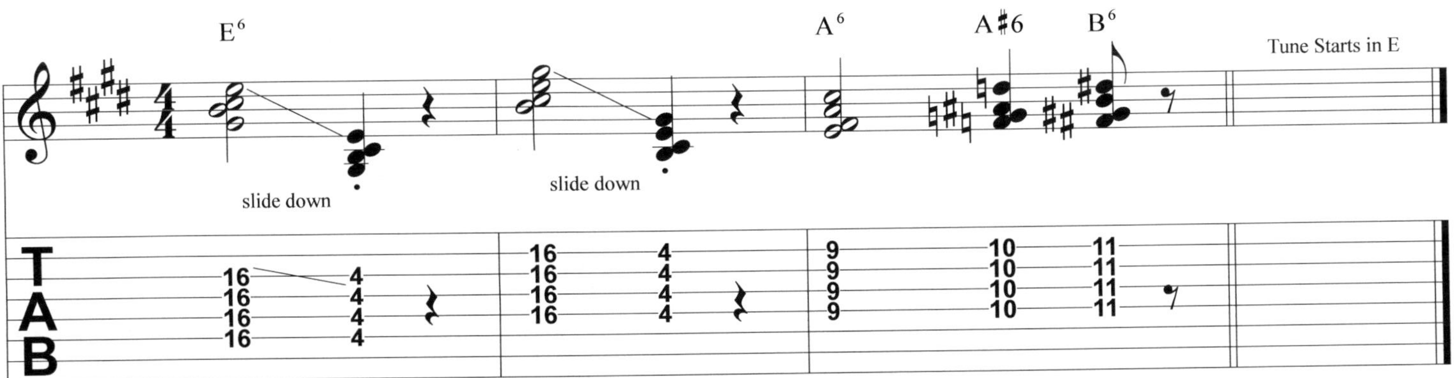

Nashville Number Chart

Note the split bar. The little dots above the chords signify the number of beats each chord gets.

4/4 1 1 4/4#/5 N/C

Lick Using 6th to 7th

The measures in A in the music below use the 6th to 7th licks. You can play them either by moving the bar, or with a string pull on the fourth string.

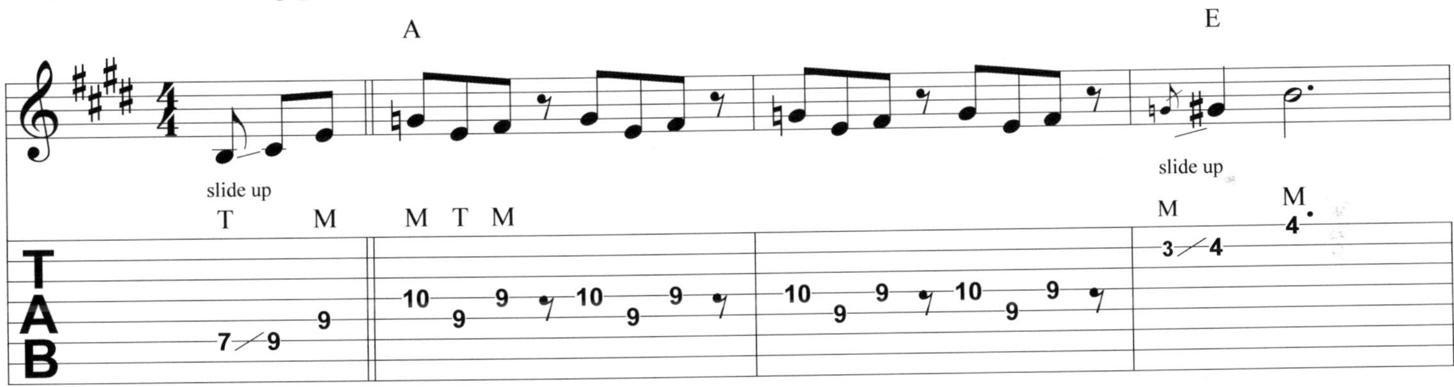

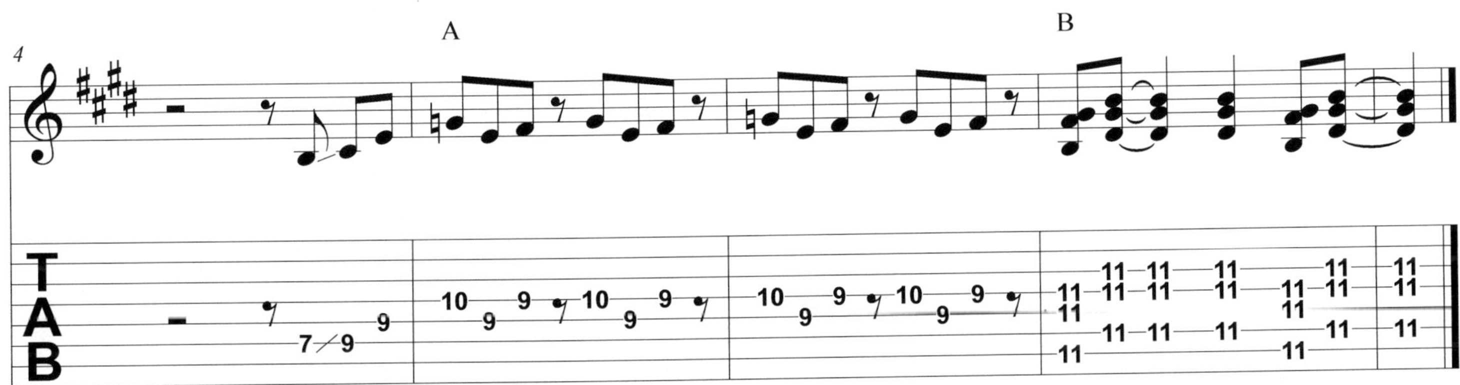

4 4 1 1
4 4 5 5

Volume Pedal Technique 

Sometimes beginners use incorrect volume pedal technique. The pedal allows you to play from soft to loud, so you need to start with the volume pedal at a moderate level. Then, pick the note and use the volume pedal to give it sustain by barely pressing it down. The video shows this concept in better detail.

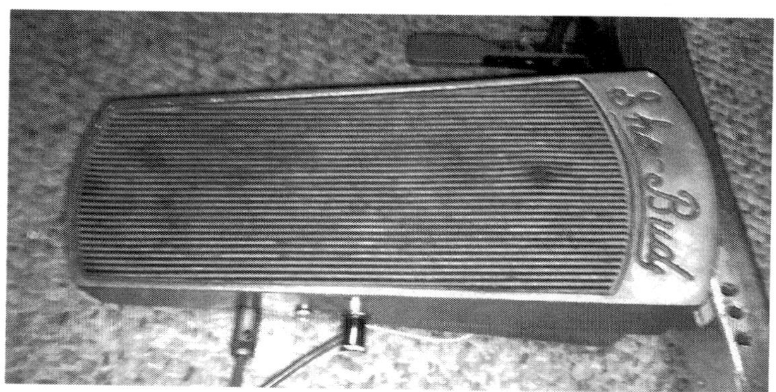

This Harmony lap steel is very similar to the Gibson EH-125.

"I think Gibson had a lot of those pickup covers left over after they went to the P-90 in 1946. There are some notations in the shipping ledgers about selling pickups to Harmony. It's possible that they sold the whole bridge/pickup assemblies to Harmony." – Walter Carter

My guess is this guitar is from the late 1940s or early 1950s.

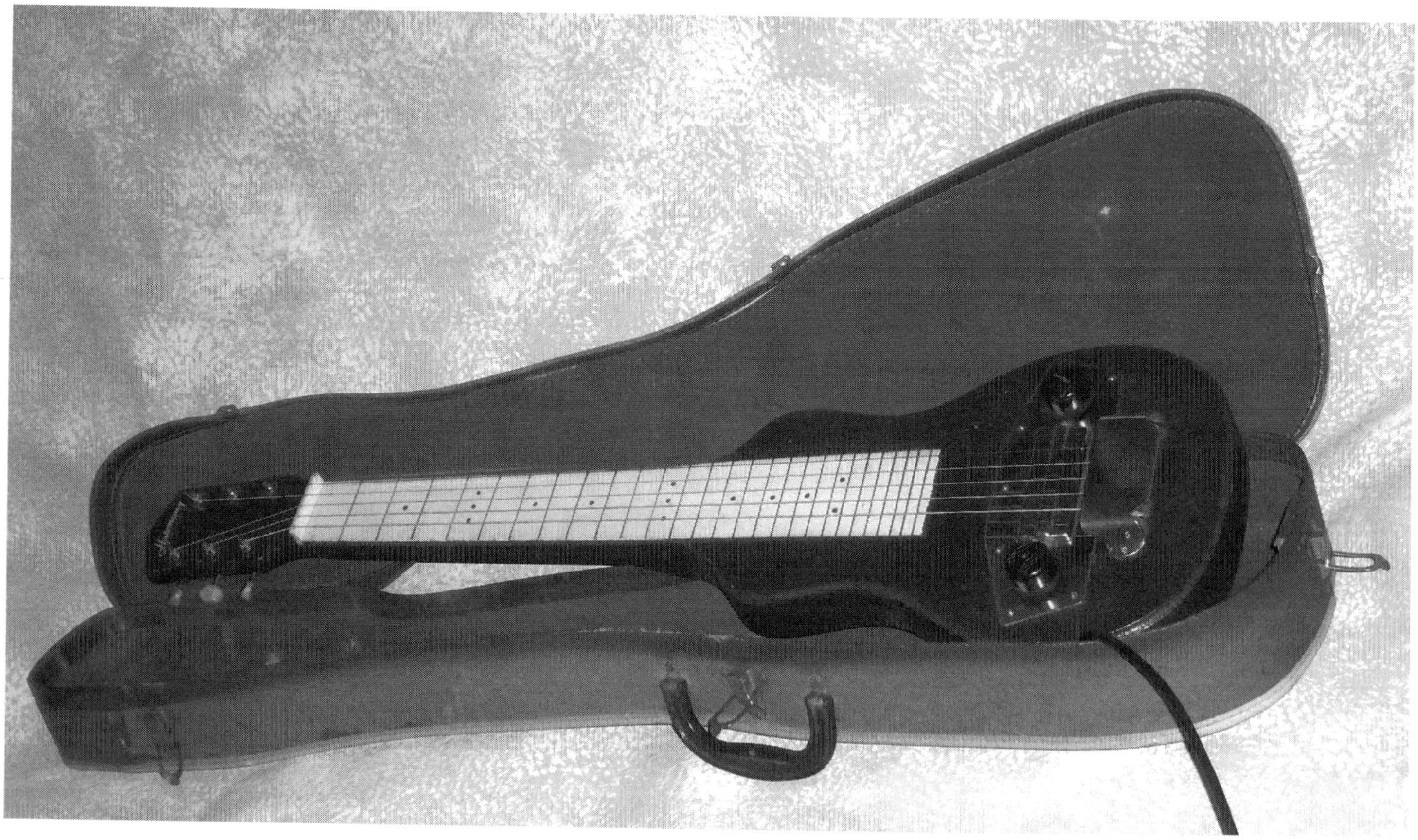

Boogie Woogie Lick

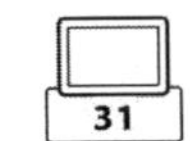

Besides being a good lick to learn, it's also a great right-hand exercise. Using the right-hand palm, the notes can be partially or fully muted.

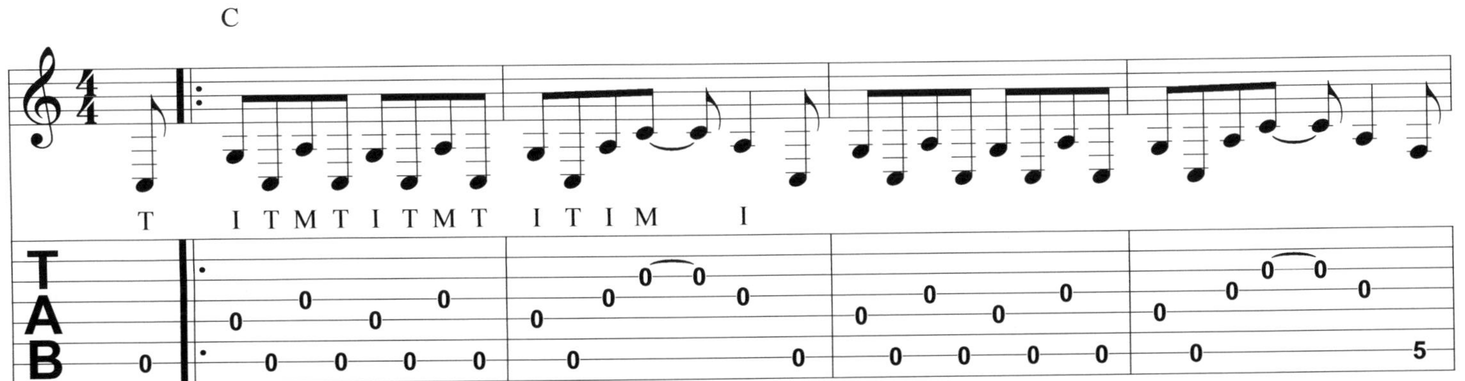

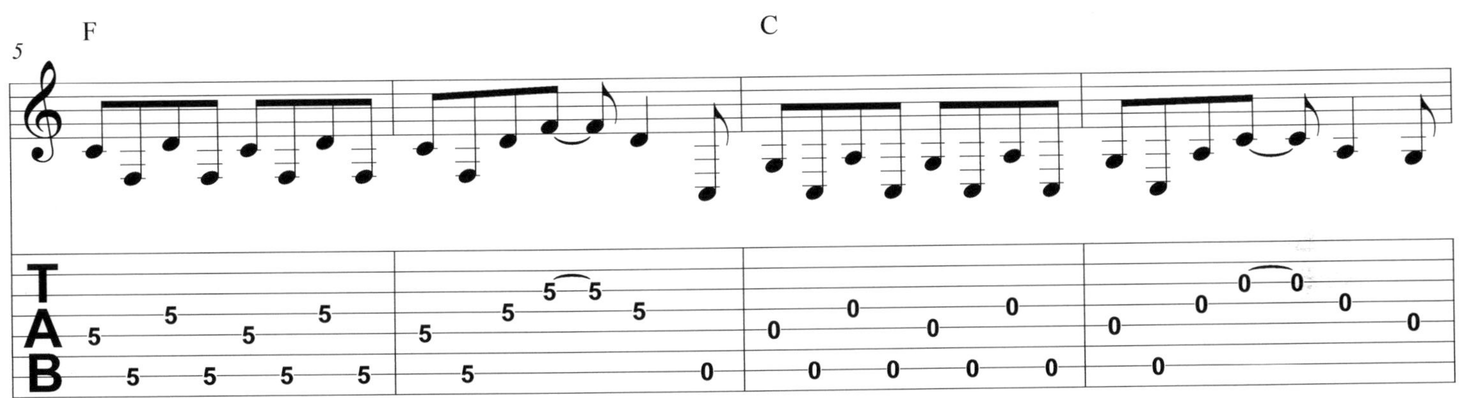

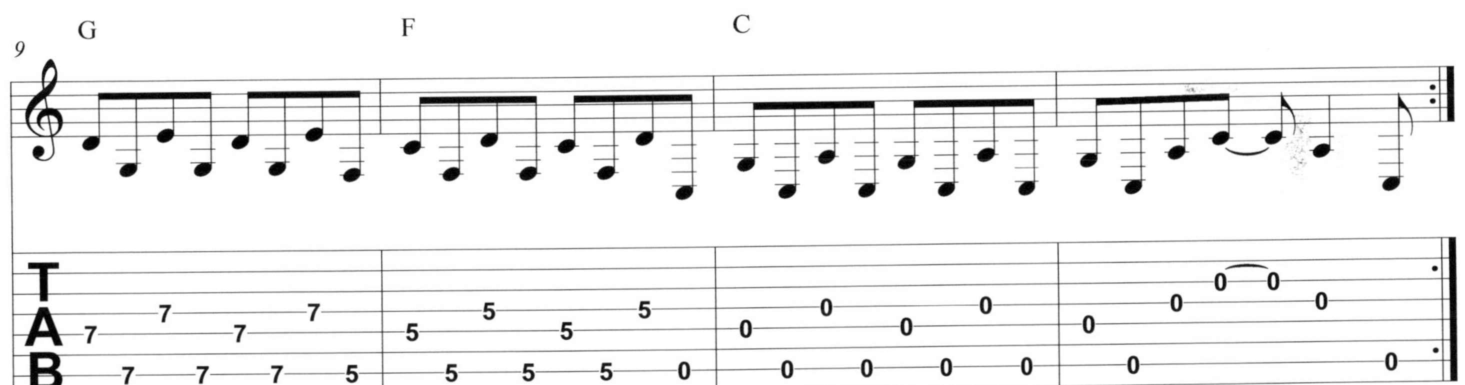

The number chart looks like this:

|: 1 1 1 1
4 4 1 1
5 4 1 1 :|

Practice this lick in different keys. You can also change up the chords and patterns and make up your own variations. Here is the boogie-woogie lick in the key of G.

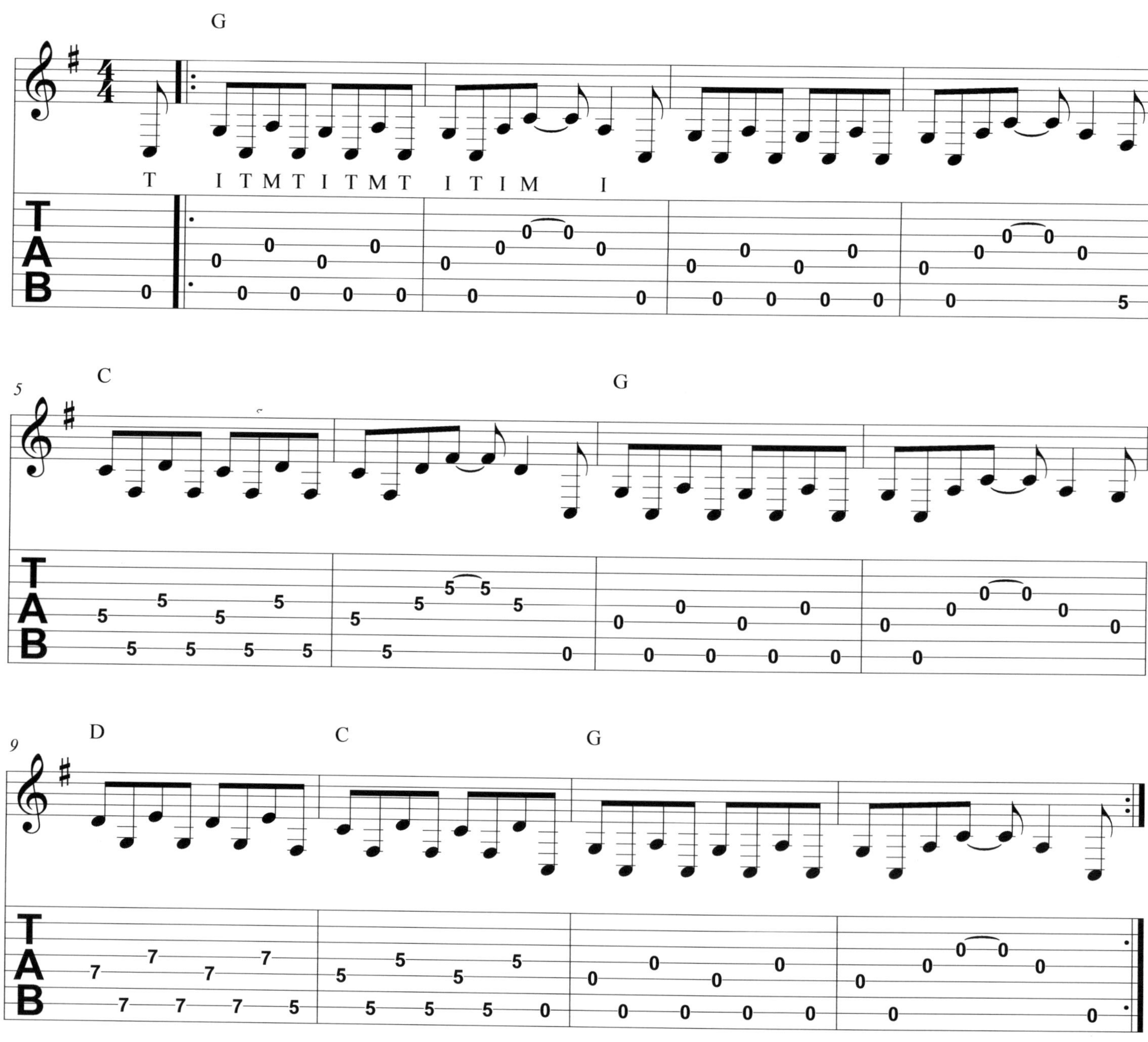

Backward Rake

This technique is somewhat advanced and will take some practice. Using the index finger of the right hand, rake down the strings and end up on the low D, 5th string. At the same time, the left hand pulls the bar back towards the low D, so each string gets muted and every note sounds briefly. Use the palm of the right hand to mute the low D immediately. In the music, that low D has a little dot under it meaning it is played staccato. "Staccato" means the note is played with shortened duration, followed by silence. After you hit this backward "rake" lick, just about anything can follow that sounds good. While I wrote the notes in the rake before the low D as grace notes, there are other ways it could have been written. Just keep in mind, it will take some effort and practice for the right and left hands to play the rake in one fluid, smooth motion.

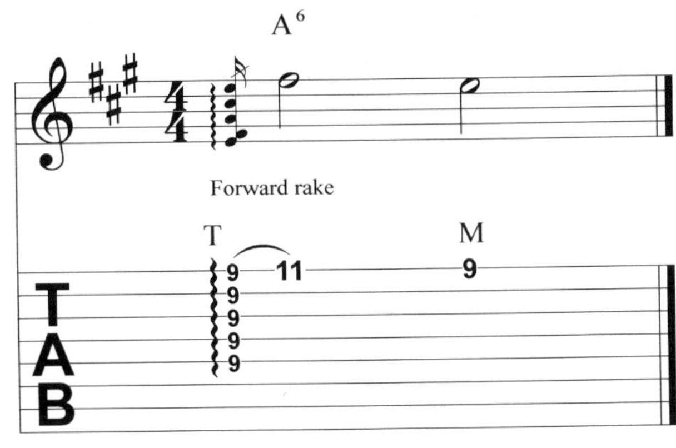

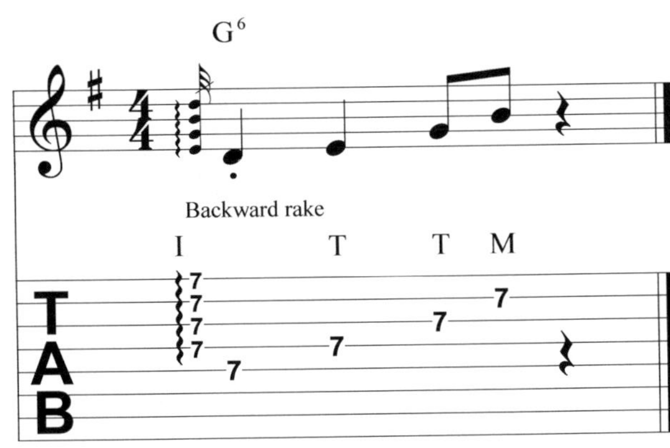

Here's another similar rake effect, except you end up on the low G, 7th fret. The rake technique in the rake is the same. After the rake, I put in a little octave lick with the G notes, with all of the low G notes played staccato.

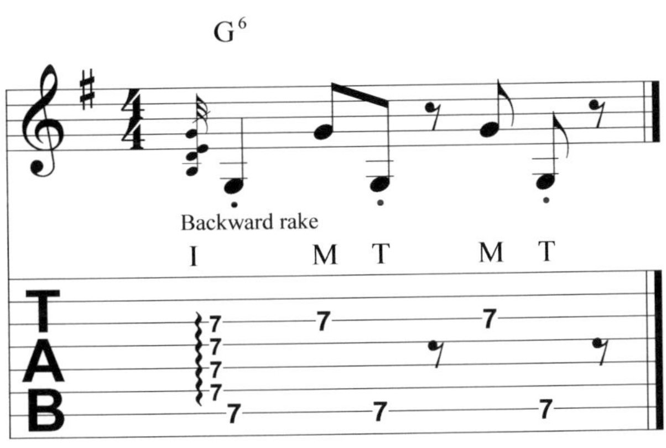

Forward Rake

Of course the forward rake technique is opposite from the backward rake because the strings are "raked" with a forward motion. This technique is inspired by Dobro® or resophonic guitar playing. In general, string blocking on the steel guitar is done by the palm of the right hand. The bar stays down on the strings. On the Dobro®, string blocking is done by picking up the bar with the left hand. That's why most Dobro® players prefer a Stevens-style bar. It's easier to lift up and come back down on the strings with a Stevens-style bar.

To play this lick, rake the strings up (forward) with the right-hand thumb, while picking (low) end of the bar up as the notes ring to cut them off. The bullet or round part of the bar stays on the first string. This is the Dobro®-style technique. Rake forward to the high E note on the first string. At this point the E should be the only note ringing. Slide up two frets to F♯. It can be a slow slide up, then back down to E. Both the F♯ and E sound good with vibrato.

A 1941 Epiphone Electar Century – Recently Epiphone released a new Electar inspired by "1939" Century Lap Steel. The photo shows the original 1941 model.

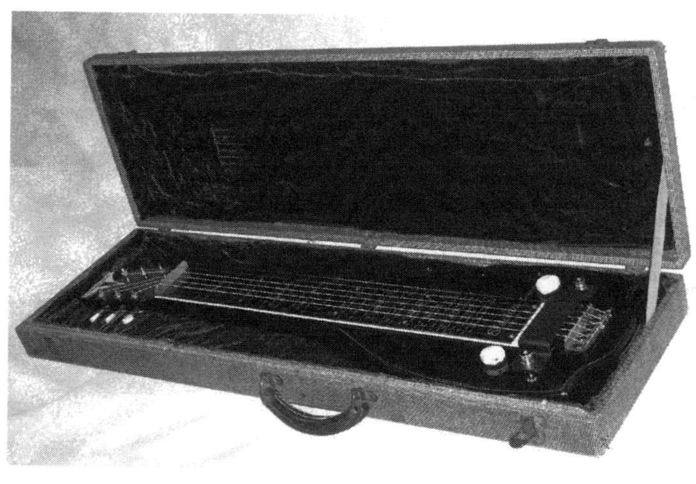

Playing Rhythm 

Most people don't consider the steel guitar to be a rhythm instrument, but I have been using rhythm techniques for years with considerable effectiveness. In the right band setting and appropriate song, they all sound great. The trick is to play softly and mute or partially mute the strings with the right palm. There are lots of different ways to do these types of rhythm licks so I'll provide a few examples.

The first example is very basic. In bluegrass music, the bass plays on beats one and three and the mandolin "chops" on beats two and four. The steel is covering the mandolin part. Don't forget to play softly, muting the strings with the right hand. Note: Avoid playing the 6th of the chord on the 4th string.

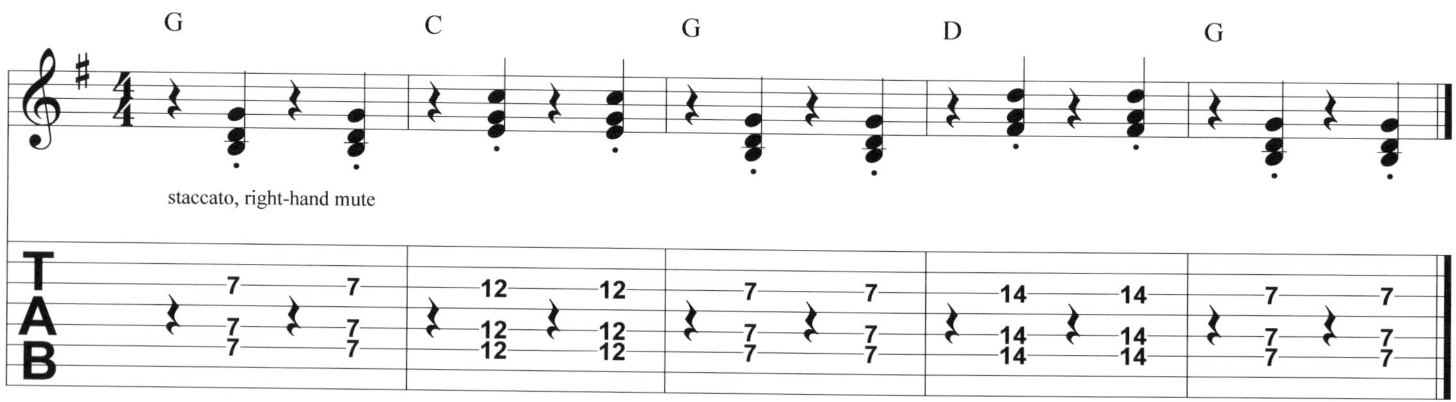

This next example just adds the bass notes.

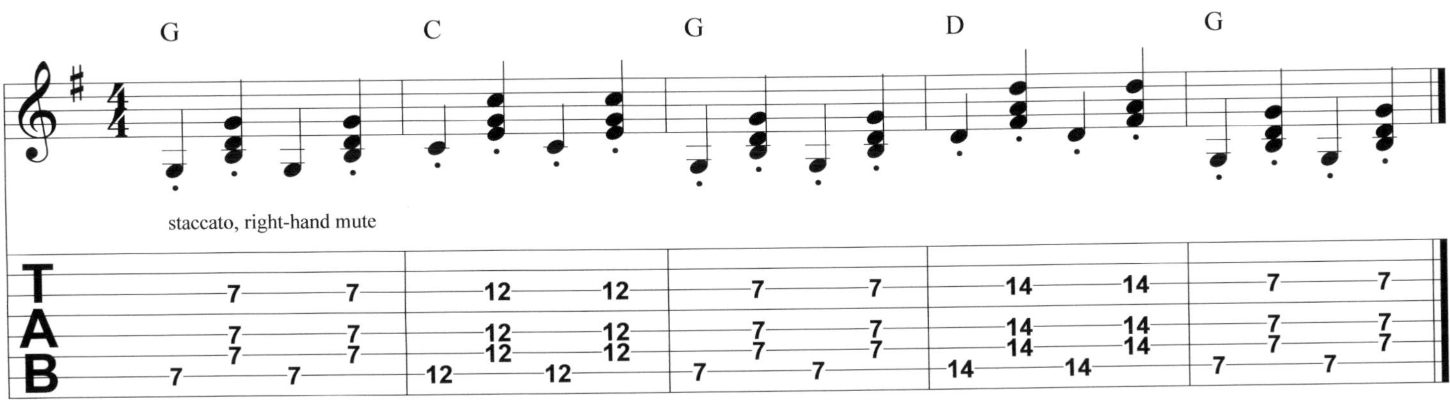

In $\frac{3}{4}$ time, here's a good accompaniment pattern, similar to what a rhythm guitarist might play.

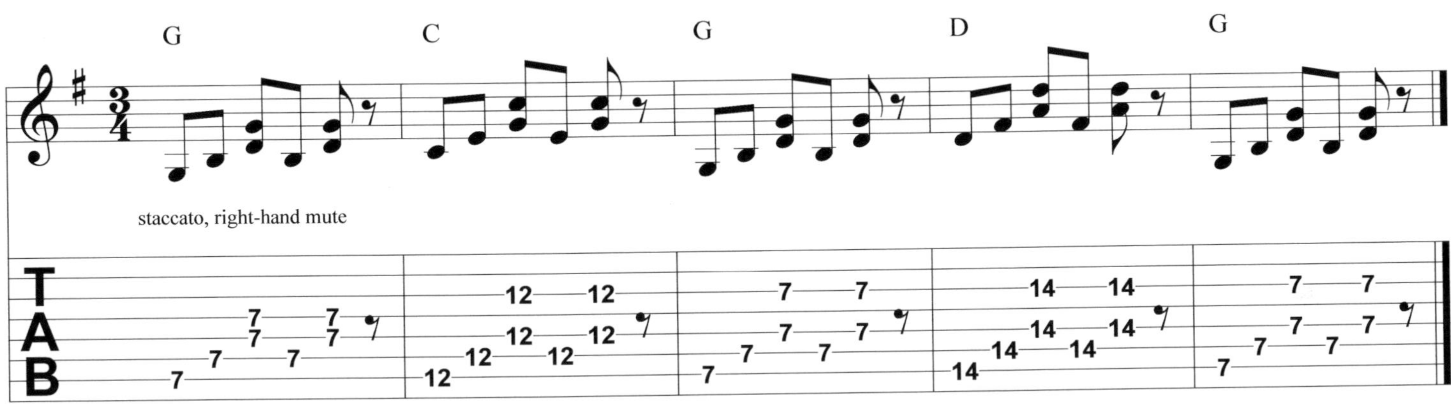

Another in $\frac{3}{4}$ time. Sometimes this is called "tick-tack" guitar.

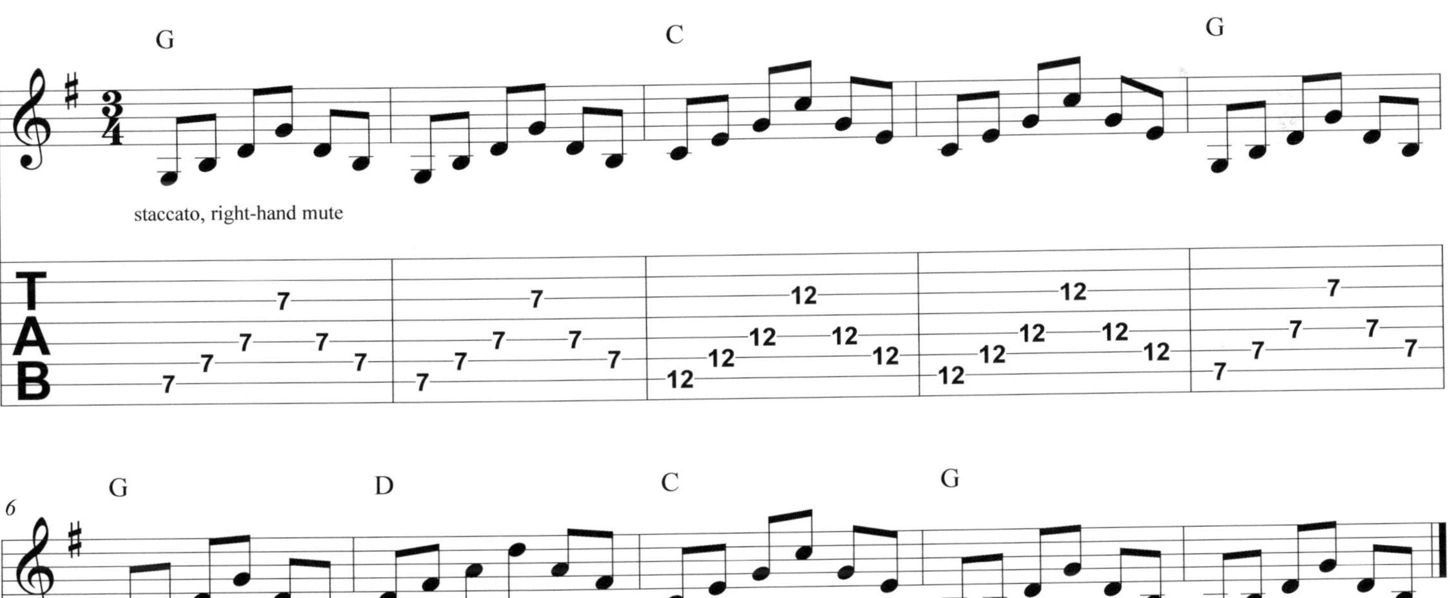

Palm Harmonics 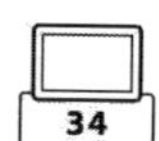

Natural harmonics, discussed previously, are great for some licks and effects, but they are limited to notes in the C^6 and G^6 chords. Palm harmonics are a little more difficult to play but all notes are available. I often use them to make chord harmonics. To play a G^6 chord, put the bar on the 7th fret. The palm of the right hand is going to lightly touch the strings of the 19th fret, an octave up the fretboard. The thumb is going to rake down on the strings and be used as a guide to position the right hand. That's the trick; it depends on the size of your right hand. I use the 5th of the chord I'm about to play, which is D on the 14th fret. And then aim approximately one fret lower, the 13th fret. But experiment, try hitting the strings on the 13th fret, go up and down a little and find that sweet spot where the harmonic sounds clear. In music notation, you might see the little diamond and 8va above a normal note head to designate a harmonic. Once you get it sounding clear, practice palm harmonics in different keys and chords.

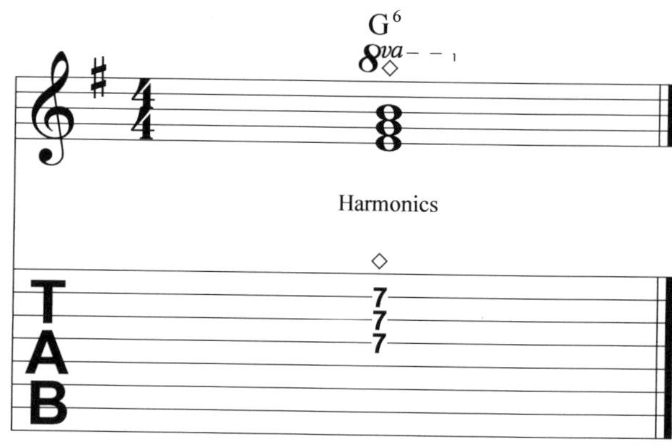

Palm harmonics work well for an ending lick, or on licks at the end of a section or phrase. On the following lick, hit the harmonic chord on the 6th fret, slide up and down twice. Then hit the 6th fret again and resolve to G^6 on the 7th fret. Here, diamond-shaped notes indicate harmonics.

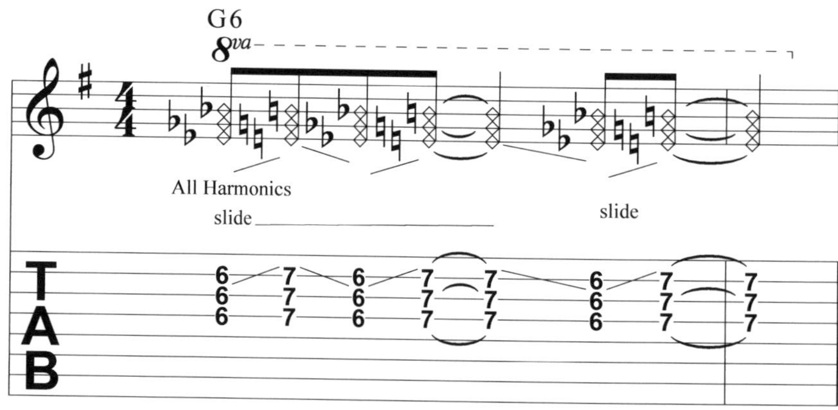

This is a common lick in western swing music. Hit the G-flat chord at the 6th fret and use the volume pedal to sound the notes. The volume goes down to up, but the volume pedal is actually going up to down to accomplish this. So you are only picking the first chord and the volume pedal and final slide do the rest.

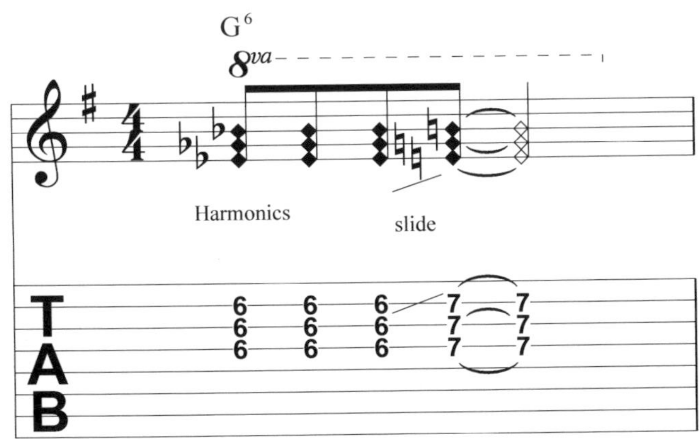

Here is a great-sounding and common lick. Hit the G6 chord and do a long, slow slide up an octave to the 19th fret. It can be used as an ending lick and played in *free time*, a type of musical meter devoid of musical pulse or time signatures.

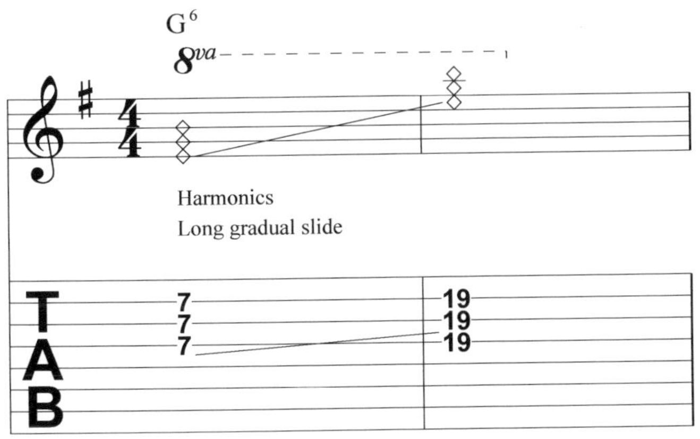

A 1947 Gibson BR-3

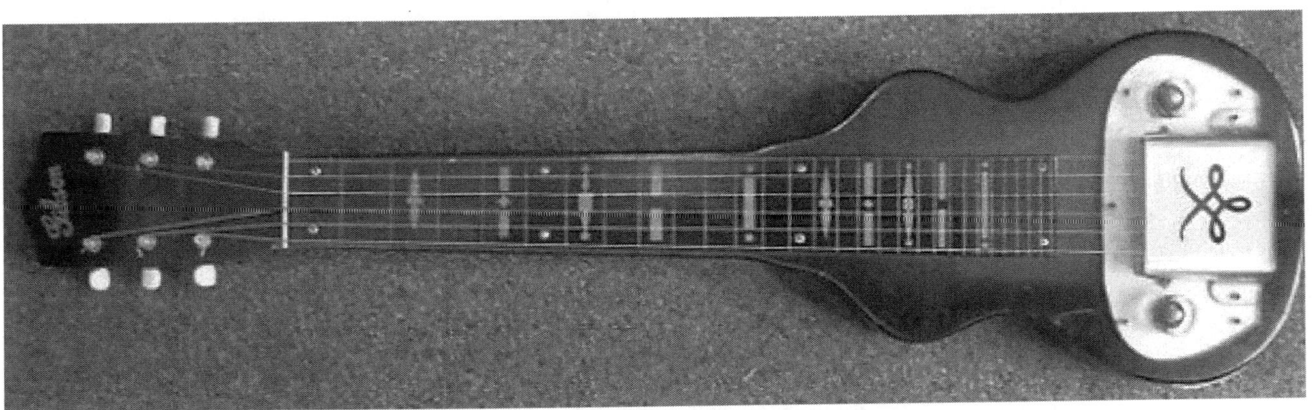

Here's an example of how harmonics using the half-step slide can be used following a lick.

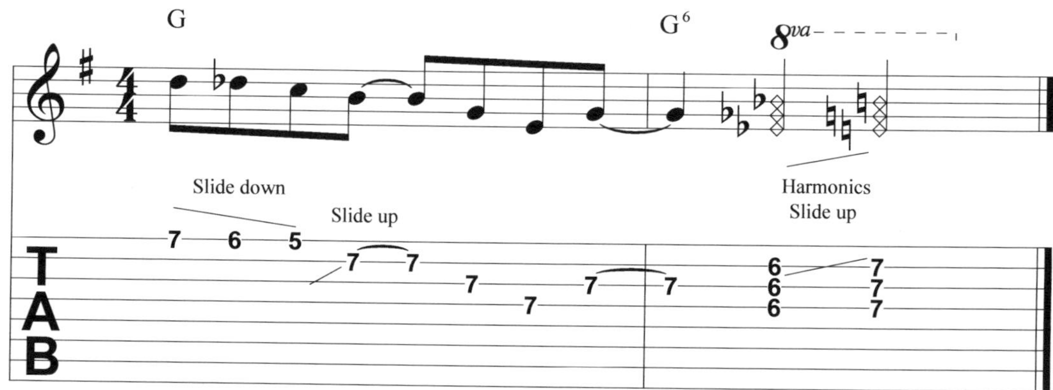

Harmonics Using the Third Finger 

Some players use the pinky of the right hand to play "pinky harmonics." I prefer to use the ring finger to lightly touch the strings while the thumb picks the string or strings. This is the most versatile way to play harmonics. You can play chords, single notes, alternate strings, slides and more with this technique. In the photo below, the bar is on the 9th fret to get an A^6 chord. The ring finger of the right hand is touching the string at the 21st fret. It's easy to position the right hand because it's up an octave from the bar.

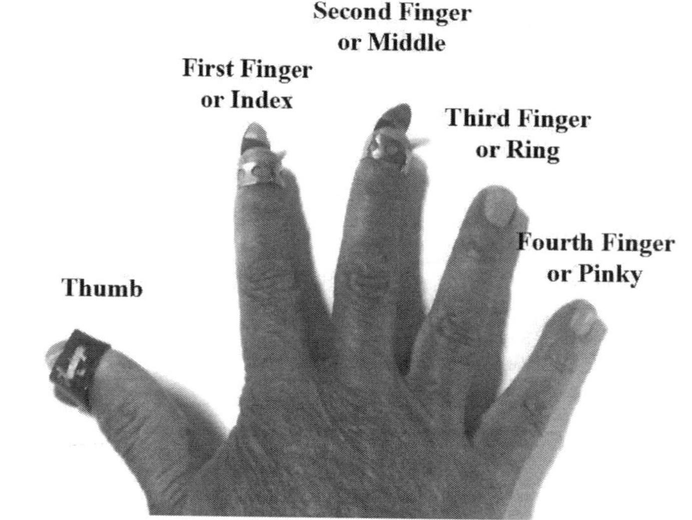

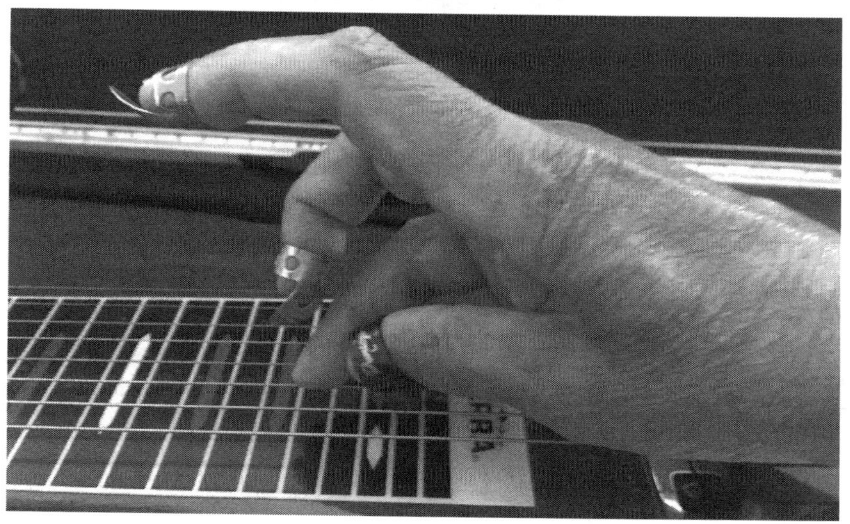

Similar to natural harmonics, you can go up to where the 5 chord occurs and play the notes in the 5^6 chord. In the key of A, that would be an E^6 chord with your mute finger on the 16th fret. And then a higher octave A^6 at the 14th fret. Here's a chart of some common keys/chords. Sure, it's a pattern—and once you learn it and practice, you will not have to think about where the mute finger goes.

Chord	Bar at	mute finger at	5 chord	higher octave
D^6	2nd fret	14th fret	9th fret	7th fret
E^6	4th fret	16th fret	11th fret	9th fret
G^6	7th fret	19th fret	14th fret	12th fret
A^6	9th fret	21st fret	16th fret	14th fret
C^6	12th fret	24th fret	19th fret	17th fret

First try playing a single note, then the following examples. Let all the notes ring as a chord. The right-hand third finger lightly touches the 19th fret. The thumb picks away from you. A little vibrato on the last note gives the chord a great sound.

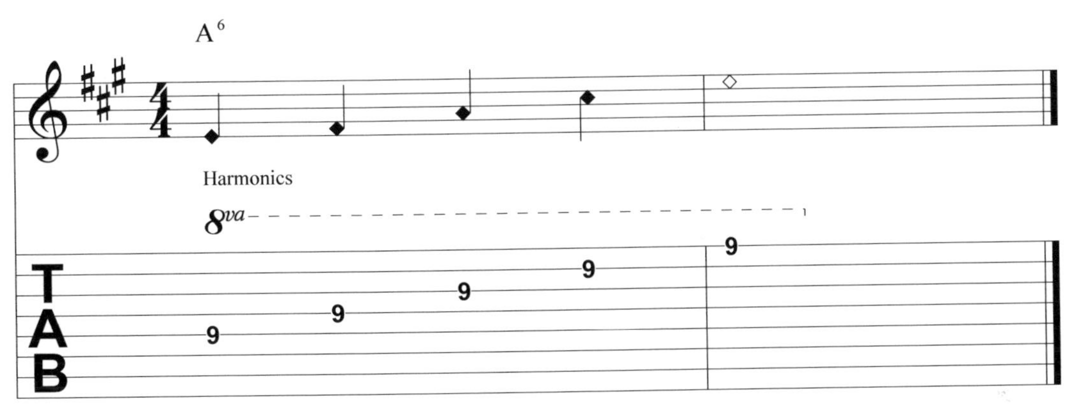

On this one, pick the strings down, up, down, etc.

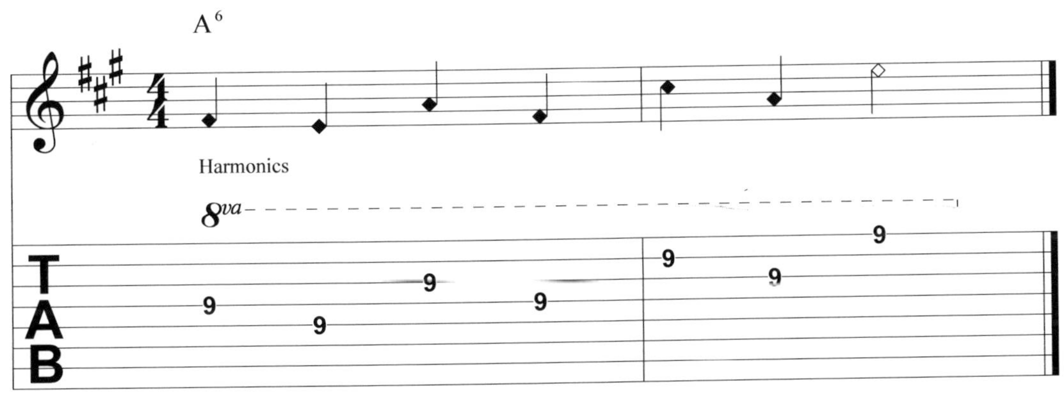

This one goes up to the 2nd string, slide the chord down one fret or a half step, and then back up.

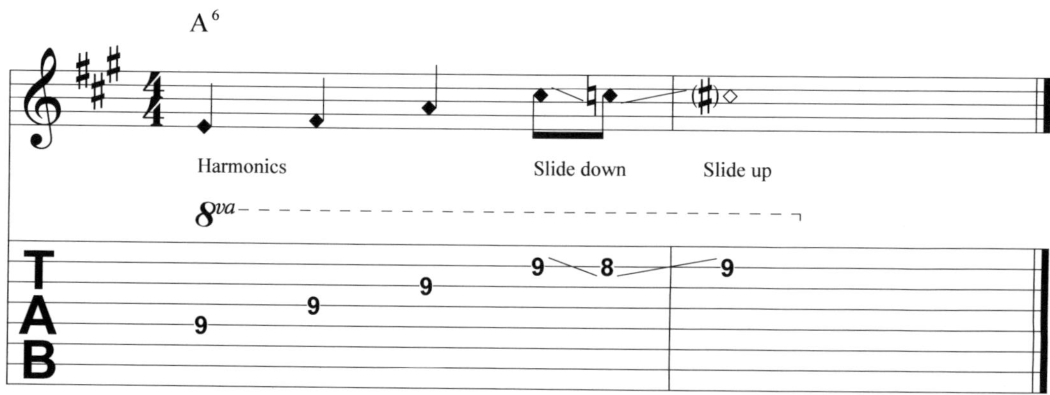

This one uses two-note chords. Rake the right-hand thumb to pick two strings at a time and remember to let all of the notes ring.

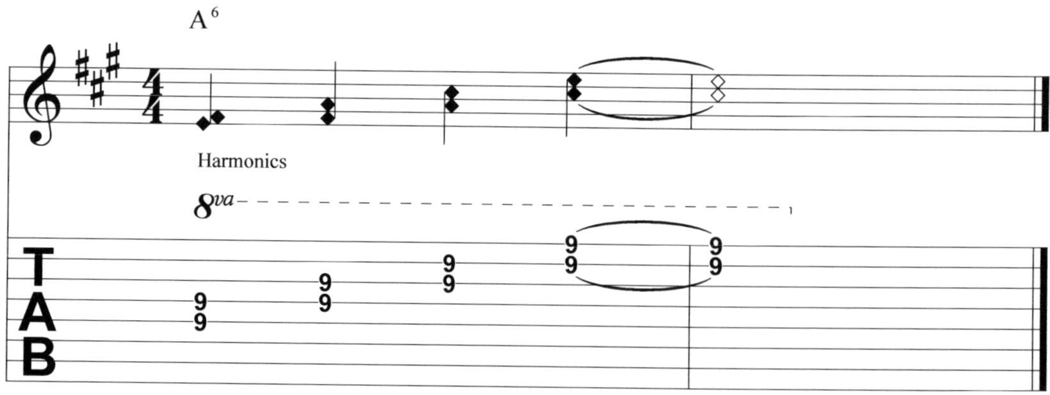

On this lick, the bar stays on the 7th fret. The tablature staff instead shows where the chime or right-hand ring finger hits.

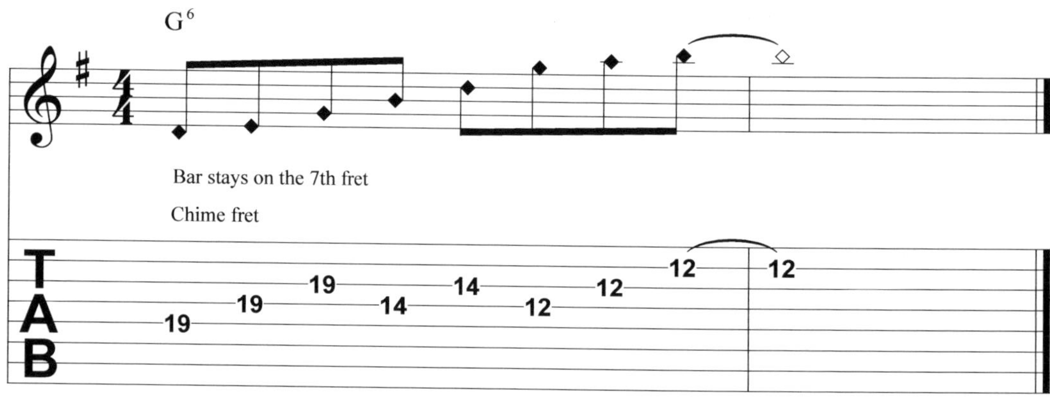

This lick demonstrates how you can use string pulls with harmonics. The C note in the first measure is not really the bar moving to the 8th fret, it's a string pull and release.

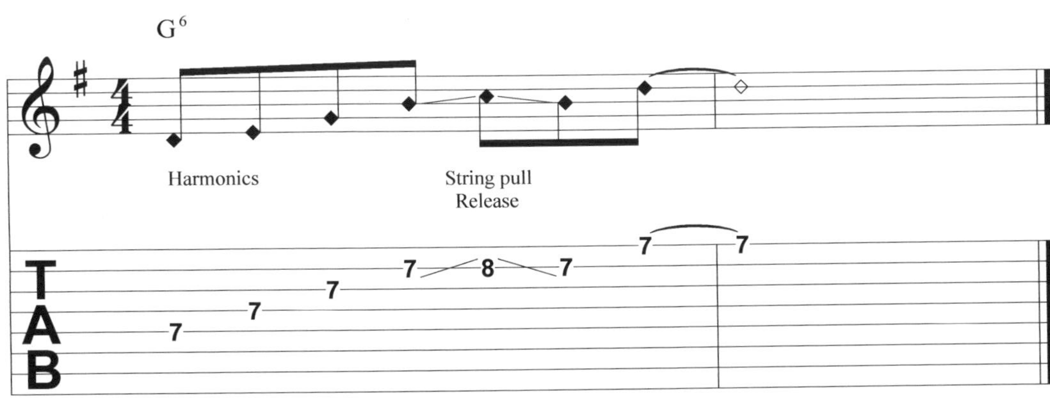

This example shows how harmonics can move between chords. Hit the D note on the 7th fret, slide up to the 14th and back down to G in the C chord.

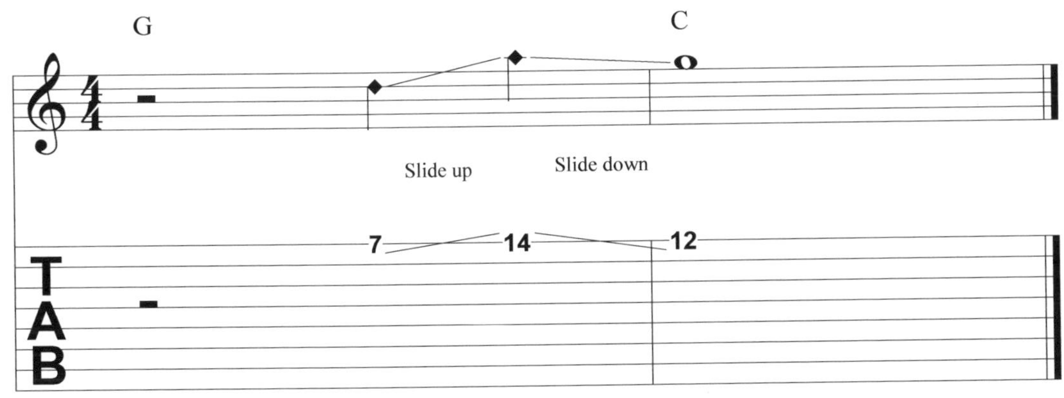

A 1952 Bronson Singing electric lap steel guitar.

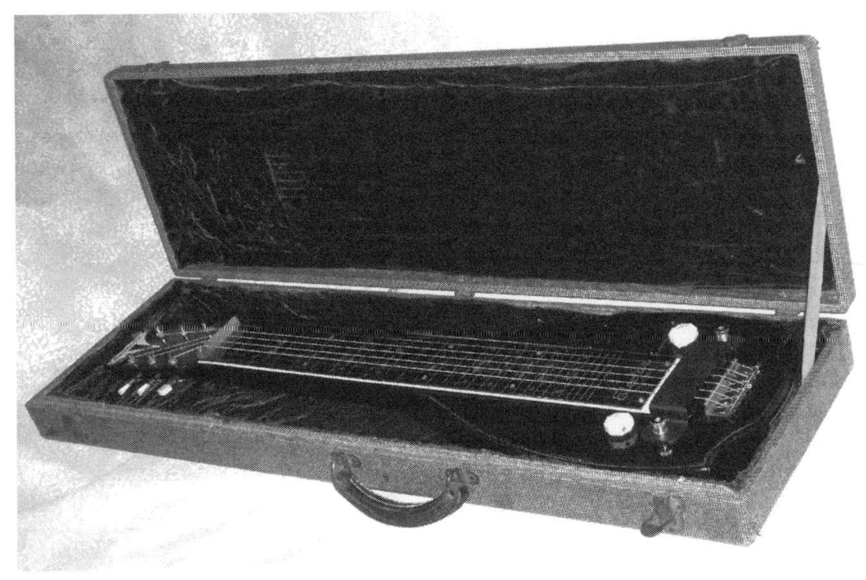

Licks that Include Open Strings 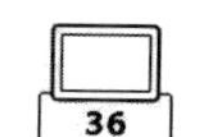

Combining open strings and bar slants can create some interesting and beautiful chords. This first one is a great example of a 4 chord changing to a 4 minor.

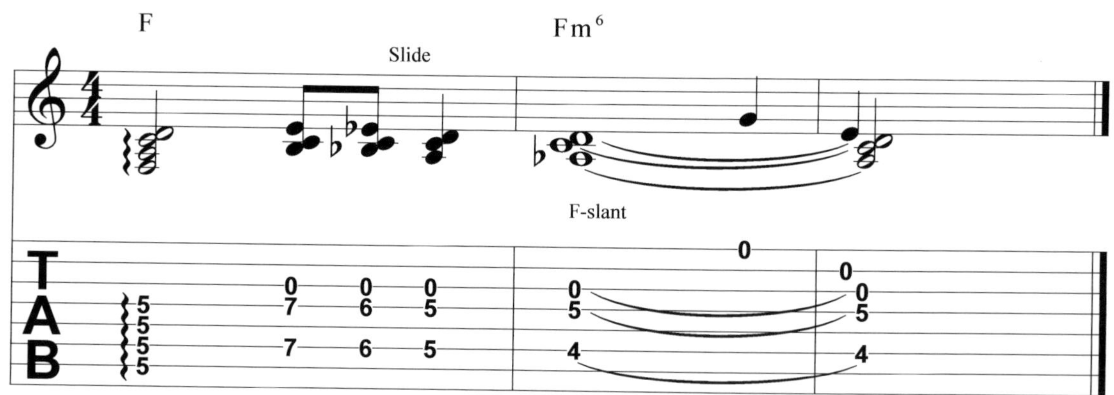

Here's another example using a nice chord progression.

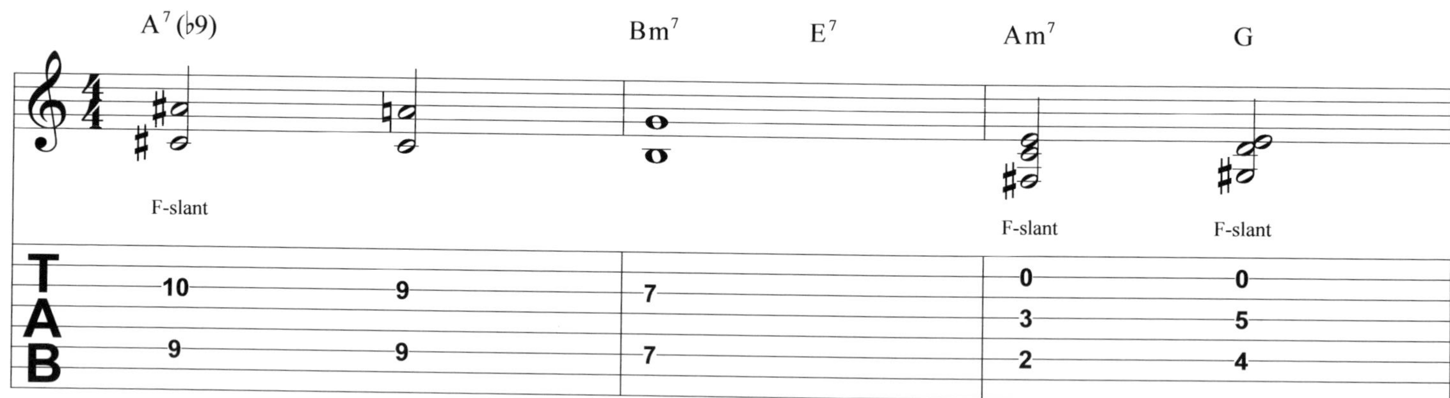

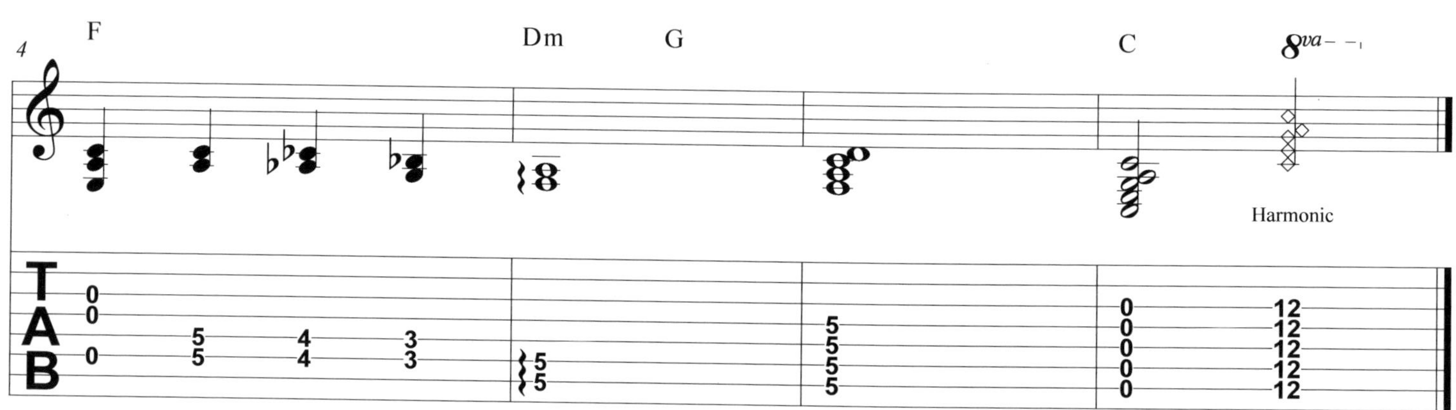

This page has been left blank to avoid awkward page turns.

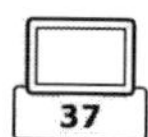

Midnight Ride

This tune adds some new items in the notation. It is written in "cut time," $\frac{2}{2}$ or ₵. It means that there are two beats to a measure, and a half note gets one beat. Don't let that scare you. It usually means the song is played at a faster tempo. Instead of counting 1-2-3-4, count 1-&-2-&, or just 1 - 2.

The other new detail deals with the "road map" of how the song is played. Think of the coda as the ending. The first measure contains three pickup notes. Play to measure 32 and D.S. al Coda. That means go back to the double bar and *Segno* (sign) at the top of the tune, play to measure 15 (To Coda) and skip to the ending marked "Coda." The words "To Coda" are often omitted.

William Bay

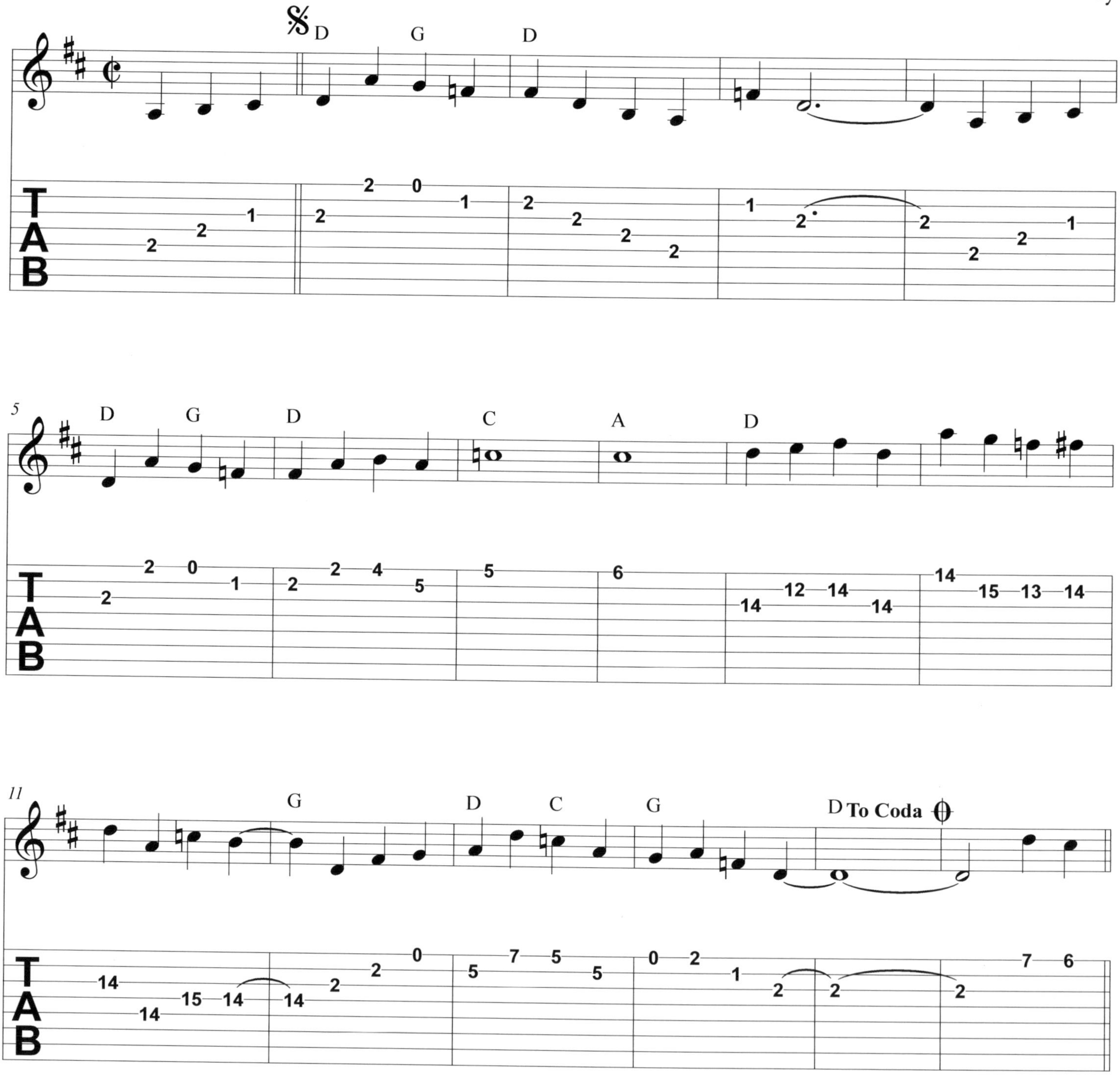

D G D

5 D G D C A D

11 G D C G D To Coda

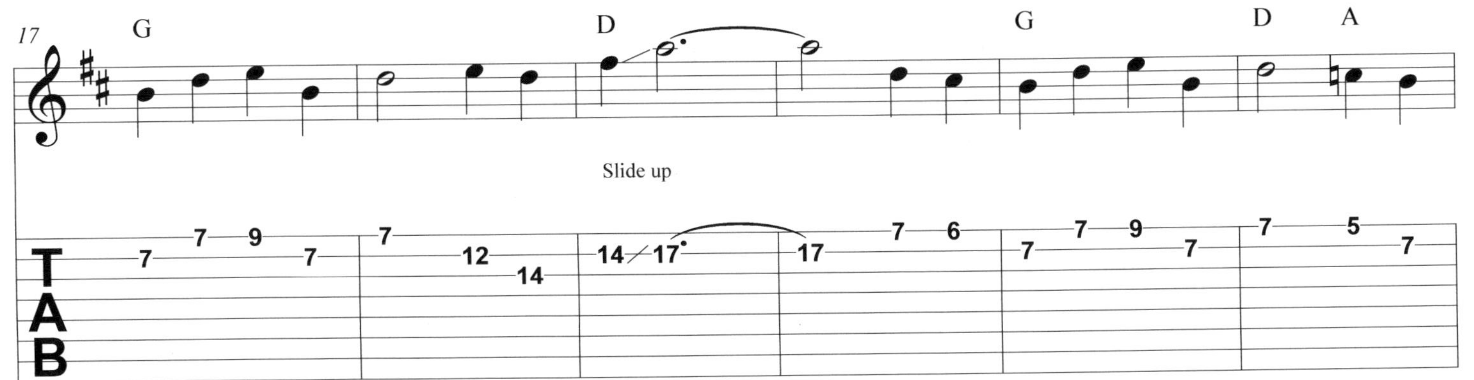
17
G
D
G
D
A
Slide up
TAB

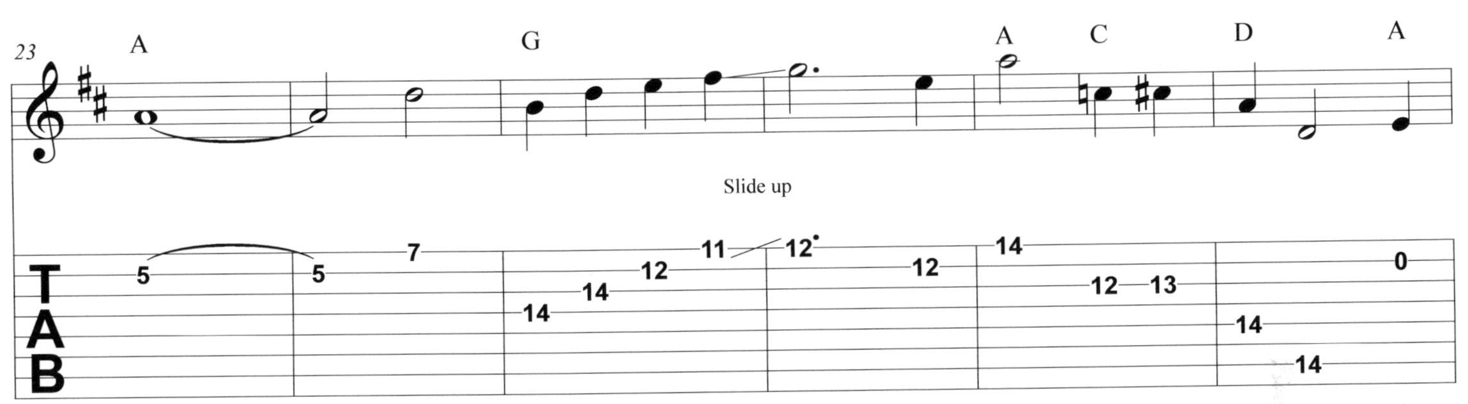
23
A
G
A
C
D
A
Slide up
TAB

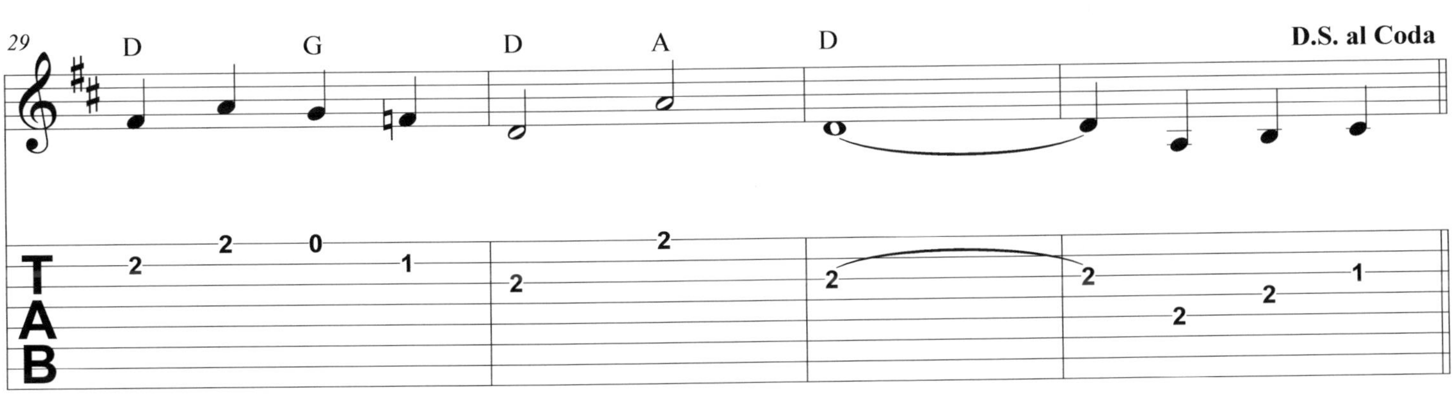
29
D
G
D
A
D
D.S. al Coda
TAB

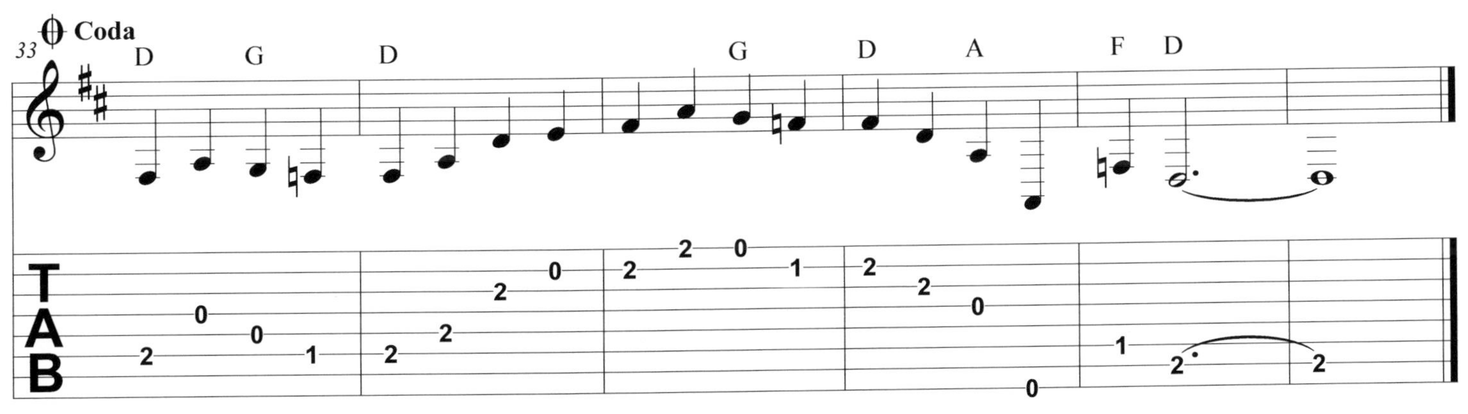
Coda
33
D
G
D
G
D
A
F
D
TAB

Why have a vintage lap steel and play it through a new amplifier? Here's a 1955 Fender Tremolux amp.

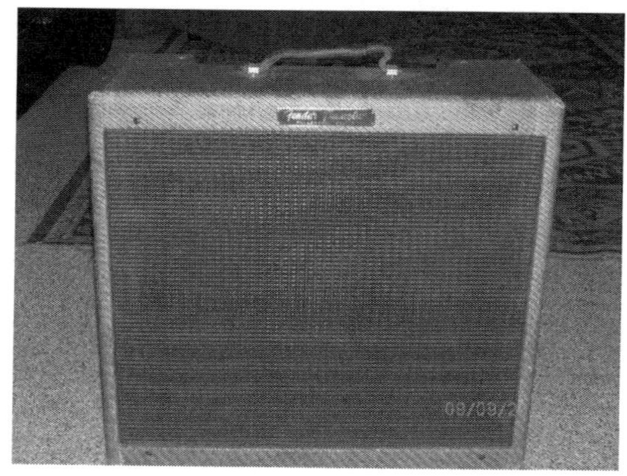

Midnight Ride

Nashville Number Chart

¢				
	1/4	1	1	1
	1/4	1	♭7	5
	1	1	1	4
			To Coda	
	1/2	4	1	1
	4	4	1	1
	4	1/5	5	5
	4	4	5/♭7	$\dddot{1}/\dot{5}$
			D.S. al Coda	
	1/4	1/5	1	1

𝄌 *Coda*

1/4	1	1/4	1/5	$\flat\dot{3}/\dddot{1}$	1

A Gibson EH-150, original case and amp.

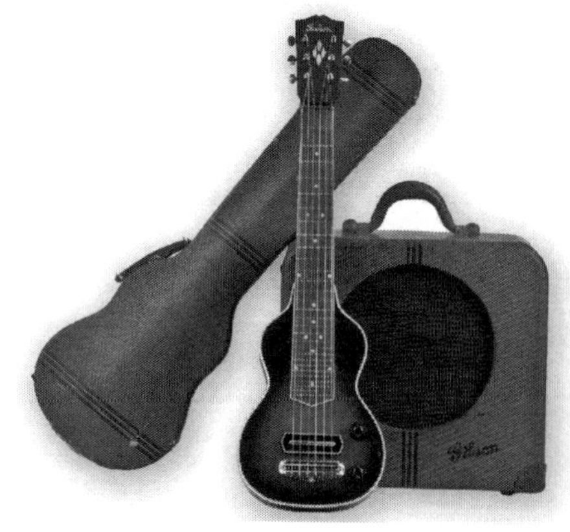

38

Lost Love

Here's a pretty song in waltz time. Feel free to "change up the tablature," that is, find different places on the fretboard to play the melody.

William Bay

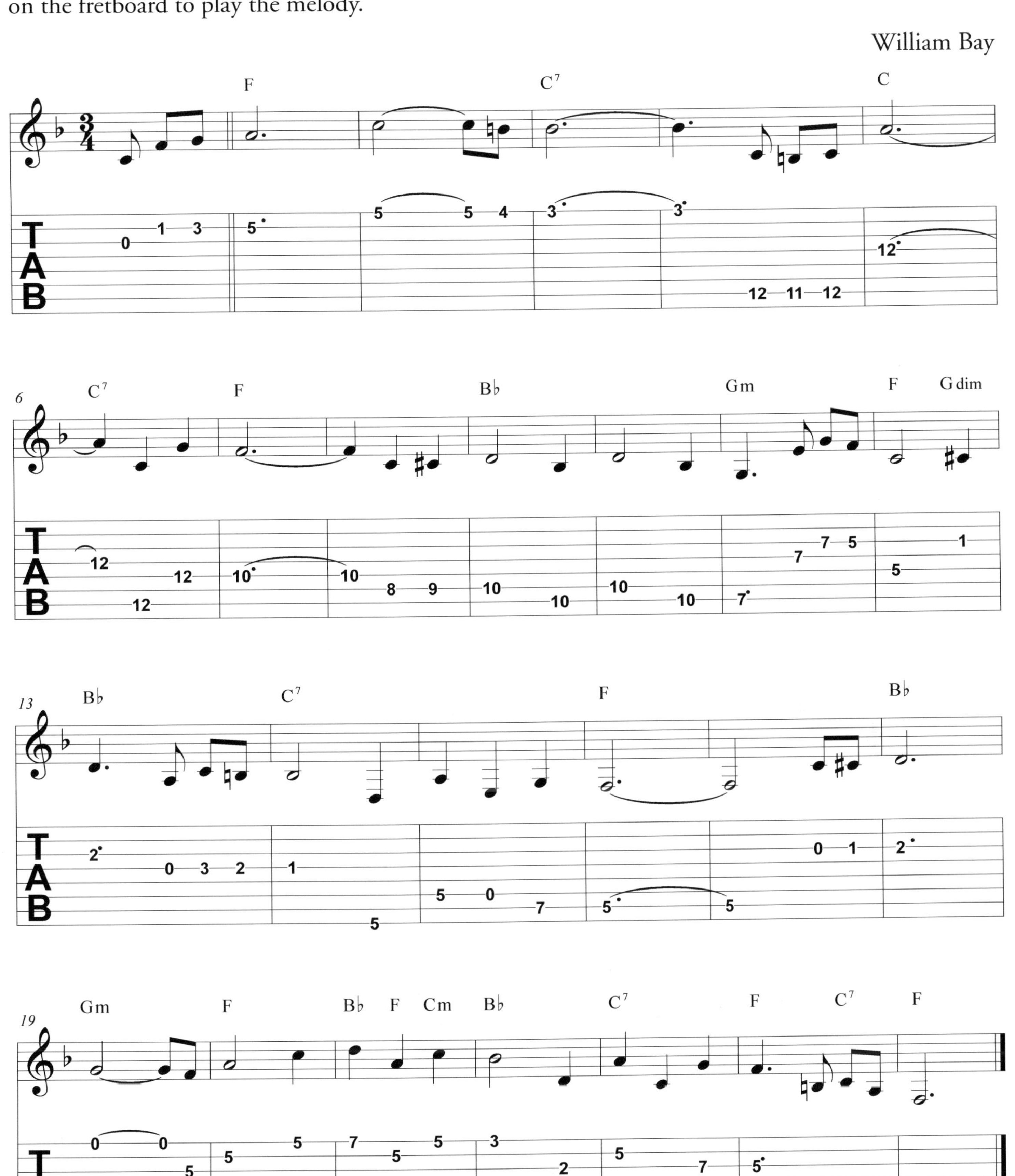

Lost Love
Nashville Number Chart

$\frac{3}{4}$	1	1	5^7	5^7
	5	5^7	1	1
	4	2^m	$\ddot{1}/\dot{2}^o$	4
	5^7	5^7	1	1
	4	2^m	1	$4/1/5^7$
	4	5^7	$\ddot{1}/\dot{5}^7$	1

Final Advice: Continue Learning

Practice or play your steel guitar every day, even if it's just for ten minutes. Play with a metronome most of the time. Practice at a slow tempo and then gradually increase the speed. Experiment with the things you have already learned; create new licks and new sounds. It's fine if you make mistakes; that is how you learn and develop your "ear." Go to jam sessions and play with others. Go out and listen to live steel players. Get together with friends and swap licks. Listen to all kinds of music online. Play different guitars and experiment with different tunings.

Remember, it's not about how fast you can play, how deep your technical knowledge is, how many notes you can put into a solo. It's all about playing with taste and being "musical." Play because you enjoy it: it's a lifelong learning process.

When you are playing in a band situation, there are some important points to keep in mind. I have been around some players that, technically speaking, are very musically gifted and can play in a very complex manner. But there are some that play with bad taste. They play too loud and/or are too "busy." That is, they play too much and never let anyone else play fills and backup. These types are no fun to pick with and very unprofessional. In a band situation, use your ears and listen to what the other musicians are doing. Take turns playing fills. Play tastefully and sparsely. Playing with great tone and tasty licks is better than playing loud with a lot of notes. A band leader gave me some good advice once. He said that nobody should play fills during the first verse or chorus unless the song has "signature" licks. Good advice! Sometimes I don't play at all on the verse and then come in playing fills on the chorus. When you take a "break" or solo, pass the second half off to someone else. All this goes a long way into having people enjoy picking with you.

For more in depth information on standard music notation I recommend the following book or e-book:

Music Theory 101

by Larry McCabe
Hundreds of musical components related to melody, harmony, and rhythm are blended together to make music. The study of these elements is called "music theory." This book explains basic theory as it relates to the needs of the average musician. It covers basic music reading with note names and time values, accidentals, ties, and other symbols and terms, as well as the theory behind the most common scales and chords. Quizzes throughout the book reinforce key concepts.

Available on the Mel Bay website: www.melbay.com

About the Author

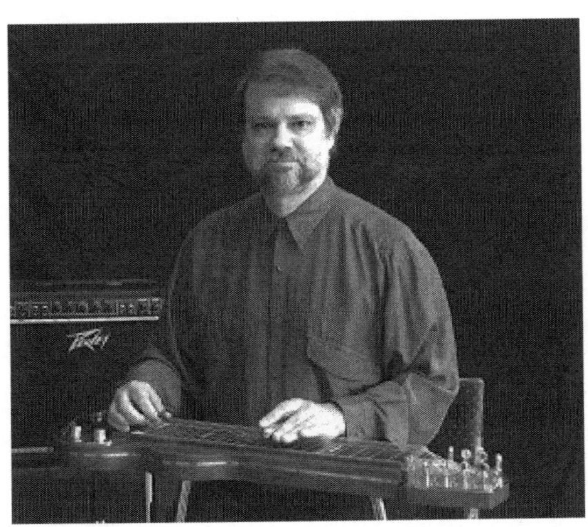

Rob Haines has been working professionally as a Nashville musician since 1982, playing the steel guitar, dobro, mandolin, and guitar. He has toured with, backed up and recorded with many well-known country artists including: Patty Loveless, Shania Twain, Lorrie Morgan, Pam Tillis, Chely Wright, Ken Mellons, Vassar Clements, Tom T. Hall, Johnny Lee, Hank Thompson, Lee Greenwood, Brenda Lee, Mandy Barnett, Louise Mandrell, Jeannie C. Riley, The Jordanaires, Johnny Russell, Fred "Too Slim" LaBour, Country Gazette and Doug Stone.

Rob played with Jeannie C. Riley's band from 1985 to 1990. From 1990 through 1998 he played in Opryland's Country Music USA show in Nashville. From 1990 to 2002 he played 1st mandolin in the Nashville Mandolin Ensemble, recording three albums including the critically acclaimed Gifts for Sony/Columbia. In 1993 Rob was a full-time member of Shania Twain's band, touring the US and Canada.

At this writing, Rob is performing with Bruce and Kristi Cline and The Music City Wranglers, Patty Mitchell and The Pickups, Trayler Parker and the Propane Tanks, Jerry Krahn's New Orleans Parlor String Band, and his own group, The Vintage Mandolin Quartet.

http://www.robhainesstudio.com/vmq.htm

Other Mel Bay Lap Steel Products

The Encyclopedia of Acoustic Lap Steel Guitar Solos
Perez

The Complete Acoustic Lap Steel Guitar Method
Perez

The Art of Hawaiian Steel Guitar
Phillips

The Art of Hawaiian Steel Guitar, Volume 2
Phillips

Don Helms-Your Cheatin' Heart-Steel Guitar Book
Helms/Scott

Acoustic Lap Steel Guitar
Funk

First Lessons: Lap Steel Guitar
Leach

Basic C6th Nonpedal Lap Steel Method
Scott

Complete Steel Guitar Method
Filiberto

Lap Steel Guitar Anatomy and Mechanics Wall Chart
Georgescu

Anyone Can Play C6 Lap Steel Guitar DVD
Haines

Mel Bay Resophonic Guitar Products

Chords and Scales for Dobro® and Lap Steel Guitar
Beanstock

Deluxe Dobro® Tune Book
Phillips

Complete Dobro® Player
Phillips

Gospel Dobro®
Eidson/Swatzell

You Can Teach Yourself Dobro®
Davis

Beginning Dobro® Solos
Phillips

Learn to Play Bluegrass Dobro®
Eidson/Swatzell

Parking Lot Picker's Songbook – Dobro®
Bruce/Phillips

Resonator Guitar Anatomy and Mechanics Wall Chart
Georgescu

A Dobro® Player's Guide to Jamming
Yaffey

First Jams: Dobro®
Andrews

The Great Dobro® Sessions
Phillips

Country Dobro® Guitar Styles
Eidson/Swatzell

Dobro® Christmas Songbook
Andrews

Dobro® Songbook
Eidson/Swatzell

Dobro® Wall Chart
Davis

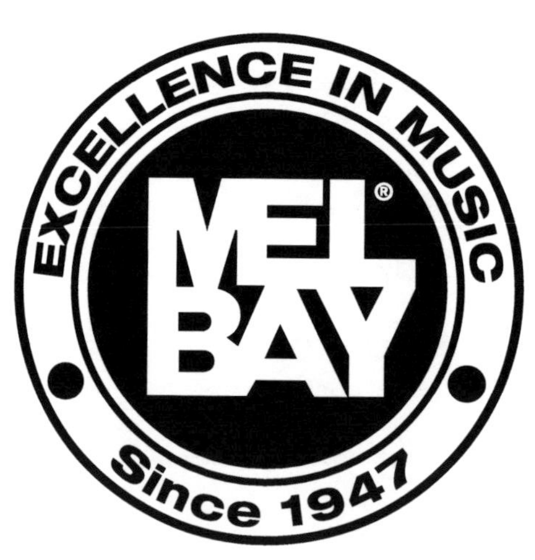

www.melbay.com